W9-BKM-277

Also by Gia-fu Feng and Jane English:

LAO TSU/TAO TE CHING

By Gia-fu Feng (with Jerome Kirk):

TAI CHI—A WAY OF CENTERING—& I CHING

CHUANG TSU
INNER CHAPTERS

PHOTOGRAPHY BY JANE ENGLISH

CALLIGRAPHY BY GIA-FU FENG

CHUANG TSU | INNER CHAPTERS

A NEW TRANSLATION BY GIA-FU FENG AND JANE ENGLISH

VINTAGE BOOKS   A DIVISION OF RANDOM HOUSE, NEW YORK

VINTAGE BOOKS EDITION, March 1974

Copyright © 1974 by Gia-fu Feng and Jane English

All rights reserved under International and Pan-American Copyright
Conventions. Published in the United States by Random House, Inc.,
New York, and simultaneously in Canada by Random House of
Canada Limited, Toronto. Originally published by Alfred A. Knopf,
Inc., in 1974.

Library of Congress Cataloging in Publication Data:

Chuang-tsu.   Inner chapters.

Translation of a portion of Nan-hua chen ching.   I.   Title.
[BL1900.C5F38   1974b]   299'.5148'2   73–20292
ISBN 0–394–71990–5

Cover photograph by Jane English.
Cover design by Clint Anglin.
The photograph of Jane English on page 163 is by Sue Blacker.

Manufactured in the United States of America

CONTENTS

CHUANG TSU

Very little is known about Chuang Tsu and that little is inextricably woven into legend. It is said that he was a contemporary of Mencius, an official in the Lacquer Garden of Meng in Honan Province around the fourth century B.C. Chuang Tsu was to Lao Tsu as St. Paul was to Jesus and Plato to Socrates. He developed the doctrines of Taoism with rigorous logic. His fables and humor are imaginative and poetic, reflecting a brilliant and original mind. He advocated relativity with regard to all standards and values. He is at once a mystic and a revolutionary.

The rhythm of life and its organic vision, an idea poetically implied by Lao Tsu, is brought to perfect expression in the writings of Chuang Tsu. While the other philosophers were busying themselves with the practical matters of government and rules of conduct, Chuang Tsu transcended the *whang cheng,* the illusory dust of the world—thus anticipating Zen Buddhism and laying the metaphysical foundation for a state of emptiness or ego transcendence. With imagery and fantasy, he captures the depth of Chinese thinking.

The seven "Inner Chapters" presented in this translation are accepted by scholars as being definitely the work of Chuang Tsu. Another twenty-six chapters are of questionable origin; they are interpretations and developments of his teaching and may have been added by later commentators.

CHUANG TSU
INNER CHAPTERS

道逍遥

CHAPTER ONE

HAPPY WANDERING

北冥有魚其名為鯤鯤之大不知其幾千里也
化而為鳥其名為鵬鵬之背不知其幾千里也怒而
飛其翼若垂天之雲是鳥也海運則將徙於南冥
南冥者天池也齊諧者志怪者也諧之言曰鵬之
徙於南冥也水擊三千里摶扶搖而上者九萬里
去以六月息者也野馬也塵埃也生物以息相吹也
天之蒼蒼其正色邪其遠而無所至極邪
其視下也亦若是則已矣且夫水之積也不厚
則其負大舟也無力覆杯水於坳堂之上則芥為之舟
置杯焉則膠水淺而舟大也風之積也不厚則其負大翼也無力
故九萬里則風斯在下矣而後乃今培風背負青天而莫之夭閼者
而後乃今將圖南

In the Northern Ocean there is a fish called Kun which is many thousand li in size. It changes into a bird named Peng whose back is many thousand li in breadth. When it rises and flies, its wings are like clouds filling the sky.

When this bird moves across the ocean, it heads for the South Sea, the Celestial Lake. In Chi Hsieh's record of wonders it says: "When Peng is heading toward the Southern Ocean it splashes along the water for three thousand li. It rises with the wind and wings its way up to ninety thousand li; it flies for six months, and then it rests." Heat shimmers in the air like galloping horses, dust floats like the morning mist, and living creatures are blown about in the sky.

The sky is blue. Is that really so? Or does it only look blue because it stretches off into infinity? When Peng looks down from above, it will also seem blue. A large boat draws a great deal of water. Pour a cup of water into a hollow in the ground, and a mustard seed can float there like a little ship. Place the cup in it, and it will not move, because the water is shallow and the boat is large. Only at a certain height is there enough air space for a great wingspan. So Peng rises to ninety thousand li, and there is enough air below him. Then he mounts the wind, and with the blue sky at his back, and nothing in his way, he heads for the south.

蜩與學鳩笑之曰我決起而飛槍榆枋時則不至而控於地而已矣
奚以之九萬里而南爲莽蒼者三湌而反腹猶果然適百里者宿舂糧
適千里者三月聚糧之二蟲又何知小知不及大知小年不及大年奚以知其然也
朝菌不知晦朔蟪蛄不知春秋此小年也楚之南有冥靈者以五百歲爲春五百歲爲秋
上古有大椿者以八千歲爲春八千歲爲秋而彭祖乃今以久特聞眾人匹之不亦悲乎

A cicada and a young dove laugh at Peng, saying, "When we try hard we can reach the trees, but sometimes we fall short and drop on the ground. How is it possible to rise ninety thousand li and head south?" If you go into the country, you take enough food for three meals and come back with your stomach as full as ever. If you travel a hundred li, you grind enough grain for an overnight stay. If you travel a thousand li, you must have three months' supply. What do these two small creatures know? Little knowledge is not to be compared with great knowledge, nor a short life with a long life.

How do we know this is so?

The morning mushroom knows nothing of twilight and dawn, nor the chrysalis of spring and autumn. These are the short-lived. South of Chu there is a ming-ling tree whose spring is five hundred years and autumn five hundred years. A long time ago there was a tortoise whose spring was eight thousand years and autumn eight thousand years. Peng Chu is a man famous for his long life. Isn't it sad that everyone wants to imitate him?

湯之問棘也是已窮髮之北有冥海者天池也有魚焉其廣數千里
未有知其修者其名為鯤有鳥焉其名為鵬背若泰山翼若垂天之云
摶扶搖羊角而上者九萬里絕雲氣負青天然後圖南且適南冥也
斥鴳笑之曰彼且奚適也我騰躍而上不過數仞而下翱翔蓬蒿之間
此亦飛之至也而彼且奚適也此小大之辯也故夫知效一官行比一鄉
德合一君而徵一國者其自視也亦若此矣而宋榮子猶然笑之
且舉世而譽之而不加勸舉世而非之而不加沮
定乎內外之分辯乎榮辱之境斯已矣彼其於世未數數然也
雖然猶有未樹也夫列子御風而行泠然善也旬有五日而後反
彼於致福者未數數然也此雖免乎行猶有所待者也
若夫乘天地之正而御六氣之辯以遊無窮者彼且惡乎待哉
故曰至人無己神人無功聖人無名

In the dialogue of Tang and Chi there is the same story: "In the barren north there is a dark sea, the Celestial Lake. There is a fish living there several thousand li in breadth and no one knows its length. Its name is Kun. And there too lives a bird called Peng. Its back is like Mount Tai and its wings are like clouds across the heavens. It spirals up to ninety thousand li, beyond the clouds and the wind, and with blue sky above it heads south to the South Sea. A quail by the marsh laughs, saying, 'Where does he think he is going? I bob up and down a few feet, fluttering among the weeds and bushes. This is perfection in flying. What is he up to?' This is the difference between small and great."

Thus, those who are wise enough to hold an official position, fair enough to keep the peace in a community, virtuous enough to be a ruler and govern a state, look upon themselves in the same way.

Yet Sung Yung Tsu laughs at them. For if the whole world praised him he would not be moved. If the whole world blamed him he would not be discouraged. He knows the difference between that which is within and that which is without. He is clear about honor and disgrace. But that is all. Though such a man is rare in the world, he is still imperfect.

Lieh Tsu rode on the wind, light and at ease, and returned after fifteen days. Men as happy as he are rare. Though he no longer needed to walk, he still depended on something. But suppose someone rides on the flow of heaven and earth and the transformation of the six elements and wanders in the infinite. On what is he dependent?

Therefore it is said, "The perfect man has no self, the holy man has no merit, the sage has no reputation."

Yao thought he would cede the empire to Hsu Yu, saying, "When the sun and moon are shining, isn't it hard to see a torch? When the rainy season starts, isn't it a waste of labor to continue to water the fields? If you take over, the empire will be well ruled. I am now the ruler, and I feel inadequate. May I give the empire into your care?"

Hsu Yu said, "You are ruling the empire and the world is already at peace. If I took your place, I would be doing it for the name. Name is only the shadow of reality. Do I want to be just a shadow? The sparrow building its nest in the deep wood occupies but a single twig. The muskrat drinks only enough from the river to fill its belly. Go in peace, my lord. I have no use for the empire. If the cook at a ritual ceremony is not attending to the food offerings, the priests and the representatives of the dead do not leap over the wine and the meat to take his place."

堯讓天下於許由曰日月出矣而爝火不息其於光也不亦難乎
時雨降矣而猶浸灌其於澤也不亦勞乎夫子立而天下治
而我猶尸之吾自視缺然請致天下許由曰子治天下
天下既已治也而我猶代子吾將為名乎名者實之賓乎
吾將為賓乎鷦鷯巢於深林不過一枝偃鼠飲
不過滿腹歸休乎君子無所用天下為
庖人雖不治庖尸祝不越樽俎而代之矣

Chien Wu questioned Lien Shu: "I heard Chieh Yu telling strange stories, long and fantastic, going on and on without end. I was amazed at his words. They seemed to be as boundless as the Milky Way and had no connection with the way things really are."

Lien Shu asked, "What did he say?"

"Far away on Mount Ku lives a holy man. His flesh and skin are like ice and snow; he is as gentle as a young girl. He eats none of the five grains, but takes deep draughts of the wind and drinks the dew. He rides on clouds and mounts a flying dragon and wanders beyond the four seas. By using his spiritual powers he can protect creatures from sickness and decay, and ensure a rich harvest. I think this is ridiculous and do not believe it."

Lien Shu said, "So it is. The blind cannot appreciate beautiful patterns, the deaf cannot hear the sounds of bells and drums. Blindness and deafness are not just physical; they can be mental too. Yours is a case in point. That holy man with all his virtues looks on all the confusion of the ten thousand things as one. Because of his very existence, the world is emerging from chaos. Why should he do anything about it? Nothing can harm him. A great flood reaching the sky could not drown him. Though a great drought caused metals and rocks to melt and scorched the earth and hills, he would feel no heat. From his own substance he can create philosopher kings like Yao or Shun. Why should he bother with worldly things?"

肩吾問於連叔曰吾聞言於接輿大而無當往而不返吾驚怖其言
猶河漢而無極也大有逕庭不近人情焉連叔曰其言謂何哉
曰藐姑射之山有神人居焉肌膚若冰雪淖約若處子不食五穀
吸風飲露乘雲氣御飛龍而遊乎四海之外其神凝使物不疵癘而年穀熟
吾是以狂而不信也連叔曰然瞽者無以與乎文章之觀聾者無以與乎鐘鼓之聲
豈唯形骸有聾盲哉夫知亦有之是其言也猶時女也之人也之德也
將磅礴萬物以為一世蘄乎亂孰弊弊焉以天下為事之人也物莫之傷
大浸稽天而不溺大旱金石流土山焦而不熱是其塵垢秕糠
將猶陶鑄堯舜者也孰肯以物為事乎

宋人資章甫適諸越越人斷髮文身無所用之

堯治天下之民平海内之政往見四子藐姑射之山

汾水之陽窅然喪其天下焉

A man from the state of Sung selling ceremonial caps made a trip to the state of Yueh. But Yueh people, having short hair and tattooed bodies, had no use for them. Yao brought order to the people of the world and ruled wisely over the lands bounded by the four seas. But returning south of the Fen River after his visit to the four sages on Mount Kui, he lost his interest in the empire.

Hui Tsu said to Chuang Tsu, "The King of Wei gave me some seeds from a huge gourd. I planted them and they bore a fruit big enough to hold five bushels. I used it to carry water, but it was too heavy to lift. So I cut it in half to make ladles, but they were too shallow to hold anything. They were big, unwieldy, and useless so I smashed them into pieces."

Chuang Tsu said, "My friend, you are not very intelligent in your use of large things. There was a man from Sung who could make a good salve for chapped hands. His family had had a silk-bleaching business for generations. A traveler heard of this and offered to buy the secret formula for one hundred pieces of gold. The family gathered together to have a conference and said, 'We have been bleaching silk for generations and have earned only a few pieces of gold. Now in one day we can sell the secret for one hundred pieces of gold. Let him have it.'

"The traveler took it and offered it to the King of Wu. Wu and Yueh were at war. The King of Wu entrusted the traveler with the command of his fleet. In the winter the fleet fought a naval battle against Yueh and totally defeated it. The traveler was rewarded with a fief and title.

"In both cases, the cure for chapped hands was the same but was used differently. One man got a title, while the others are still bleaching silk. Now, you had a gourd big enough to hold five bushels. Why didn't you think of making it into a great barrel and using it to float along the rivers and lakes instead of worrying about its being useless for holding anything. Your mind, my friend, is still very cluttered with trivia."

Hui Tsu said, "I have a big ailanthus tree. Its trunk is so gnarled and full of knots that it is impossible to measure it accurately. Its branches are too twisted and crooked for anyone to measure with a compass and square. It stands at the side of the road, but no carpenter would give it a second glance. Now, your words are as big and useless; no one wants to hear what you have to say."

Chuang Tsu replied, "Have you ever watched a wildcat or a weasel? It crouches close to the ground and waits for its prey. Then it leaps up and down, first one way, then the other, until it catches and kills its prey. Then again there is the yak, as great as a cloud shadowing the sky. Big as it is, it cannot catch a mouse. Now, you have this giant tree and are concerned that it is useless. Why don't you plant it on land where nothing grows, in a wild barren place? There you may saunter idly around it, doing nothing, and lie down to sleep beneath its boughs. No one will try to cut it down. Nothing can harm it since it has no use. How can it cause you any anxiety?"

齐物论

CHAPTER TWO

THE EQUALITY
OF ALL THINGS

Nan Kuo Tsu Chi sat leaning on a low table, gazing at the heavens and sighing; he appeared to be in a trance. His disciple Yen Cheng Tsu Yu, who was standing beside him, exclaimed, "What is this? Can you really make your body like dry wood and your mind like dead ashes? The man leaning on the table is not the one who was here a moment ago."

Tsu Chi said, "Yen, it is good that you asked that. Just now I lost myself. Do you understand? Perhaps you have heard the music of man but not the music of earth. You may have heard the music of earth but not the music of heaven."

Tsu Yu said, "May I ask you to say more about this?"

Tsu Chi answered, "The universe has a cosmic breath. Its name is wind. Sometimes it is not active; but when it is, angry howls rise from ten thousand openings. Have you ever heard a roaring gale?

In the mountain forest, deep and fearsome, there are huge trees a hundred arm spans around, with gaps and hollows like nostrils, mouths, and ears, like gouges, goblets, and mortars, and like muddy pools and dirty puddles. The sounds rush out like water, whistle like arrows, scold, suck, shout, wail, moan, and howl. The leading notes are hissing sounds followed by a roaring chorus. Gentle breezes make a small harmony, fierce winds a great one. When the violent gusts subside, all the hollows become quiet. Have you ever seen the shaking and trembling of branches and leaves?"

Tsu Yu said, "The earth's music is the sound from those hollows. Man's music comes from the hollow reed. May I ask about the music of heaven?"

Tsu Chi said, "When the wind blows through the ten thousand different hollows, they all make their own sounds. Why should there be anything else that causes the sound?"

南郭子綦隱机而坐仰天而噓
荅焉似喪其耦顏成子游立侍乎前曰
何居乎形固可使如槁木
而心固可使如死灰乎今之隱机者
非昔之隱机者也子綦曰偃
不亦善乎而問之也今者吾喪我汝知之乎
女聞人籟而未聞地籟女聞地籟而未聞天籟夫
子游曰敢問其方子綦曰夫大塊噫氣
其名為風是唯無作作則萬竅怒呺
而獨不聞之翏翏乎山林之畏佳
大木百圍之竅穴似鼻似口似耳似枅似圈似臼
似洼者似污者激者謞者叱者吸者叫者譹者
宎者咬者前者唱于而隨者唱喁
泠風則小和飄風則大和
厲風濟則眾竅為虛
而獨不見之調調之刁刁乎子游曰地籟則眾竅是已人籟則比竹是已
敢問天籟子綦曰夫吹萬不同而使其自已也咸其自取怒者其誰邪

Great knowledge is all-encompassing; small knowledge is limited. Great words are inspiring; small words are chatter. When we are asleep, we are in touch with our souls. When we are awake, our senses open. We get involved with our activities and our minds are distracted. Sometimes we are hesitant, sometimes underhanded, and sometimes secretive. Little fears cause anxiety, and great fears cause panic. Our words fly off like arrows, as though we knew what was right and wrong. We cling to our own point of view, as though everything depended on it. And yet our opinions have no permanence: like autumn and winter, they gradually pass away. We are caught in the current and cannot return. We are tied up in knots like an old clogged drain; we are getting closer to death with no way to regain our youth. Joy and anger, sorrow and happiness, hope and fear, indecision and strength, humility and willfulness, enthusiasm and insolence, like music sounding from an empty reed or mushrooms rising from the warm dark earth, continually appear before us day and night. No one knows whence they come. Don't worry about it! Let them be! How can we understand it all in one day?

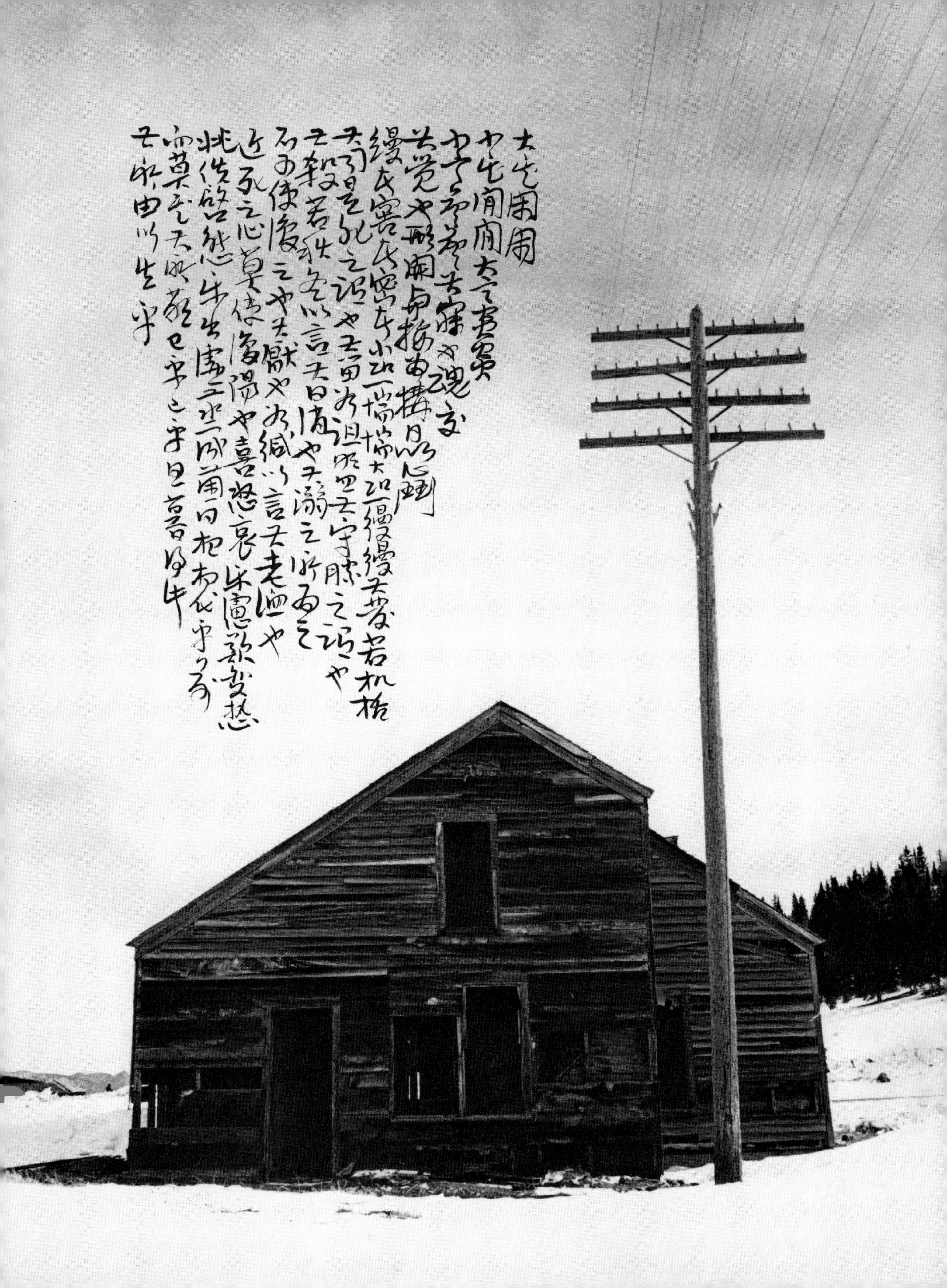

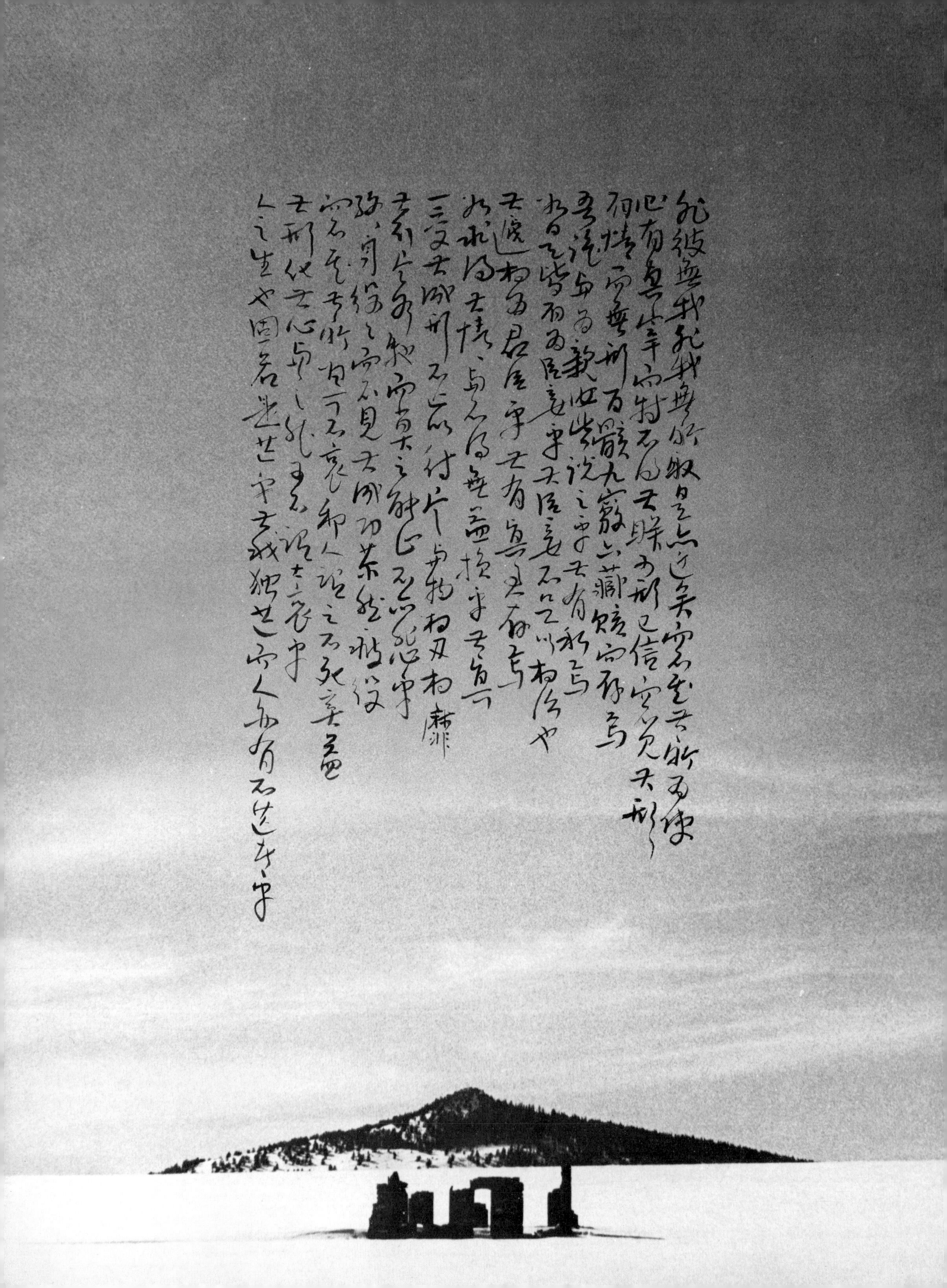

If there is no other, there is no I. If there is no I, there is no one to perceive. This is close to the truth, but we do not know why. There must be some primal force, but we cannot discover any proof. I believe it acts, but I cannot see it. I can feel it, but it has no form.

The hundred joints, nine openings, and six organs all function together. Which part do you prefer? Do you like them all equally, or do you have a favorite? Are they not all servants? Can they keep order among themselves, or do they take turns being masters and servants? It may be that there is indeed a true master. Whether I really feel his existence or not has nothing to do with the way it is. Once a man is given a body it works naturally as long as it lasts. It carries on through hardship and ease and, like a galloping horse, nothing can stop it. Isn't it sad? All through life one toils and sweats, never seeing any result. Weary and exhausted, man has no place to rest his bones. Isn't this a pity? One may say, "There is no death." What good does that do? When the body decays, so does the mind. Is this not a great sorrow? Is life really this absurd? Am I the only one who sees the absurdity? Don't others see it too?

If one is true to one's self and follows its teaching, who need be without a teacher? Not only those who are experienced and wise may have a teacher, the fools have theirs too. When those who are not true to themselves try to choose between right and wrong, it is as if they set off for Yueh today and arrived yesterday. That would be making what does not exist, exist. How do you make what does not exist, exist? Even the holy man Yu did not know how to do this, much less a person like me.

Words are not just blown air. They have a meaning. If you are not sure what you are talking about, are you saying anything, or are you saying nothing? Words seem different from the chirping of birds. Is there a difference, or isn't there? How can Tao be so obscure and yet admit of truth and falsehood? How can words be so obscure and yet admit of right and wrong? How can Tao cease to exist? How can words not be heard?

Tao is hidden by partial understanding. The meaning of words is hidden by flowery rhetoric. This is what causes the dissension between the Confucians and the Mohists. What one says is wrong, the other says is right; and what one says is right, the other says is wrong. If the one is right while the other is wrong, and the other is right while the one is wrong, then the best thing to do is to look beyond right and wrong.

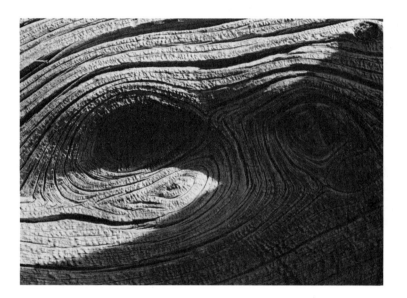

夫隨其成心而師之誰獨且無師乎
奚必知代而心自取者有之愚者與有焉
未成乎心而有是非是今日適越而昔至也
是以無有為有無有為有雖有神禹
且不能知吾獨且奈何哉
夫言非吹也言者有言其所言者特未定也
果有言邪其未嘗有言邪
其以為異於鷇音亦有辯乎其無辯乎
道惡乎隱而有真偽
言惡乎隱而有是非
道惡乎往而不存言惡乎存而不可道隱於小成言隱於榮華
故有儒墨之是非以是其所非而非其所是欲是其所非
而非其所是則莫若以明

物無非彼、物無非是。自彼則不見、自
故曰彼出於是、是亦因彼。彼是、方生之說也。
雖然、方生方死、方死方生、方可方不可、方不可方可、因
因是因非、因非因是。是以聖人不由、而照之于天
亦因是也。是亦彼也、
彼亦是也。彼亦一是非、
此亦一是非。果且有彼是乎哉、
果且無彼是乎哉、彼是莫得其偶、謂之道樞。
樞始得其環中、以應無窮。
是亦一無窮、非亦一無窮也。
故曰莫若以明。

Every thing can be a "that"; every thing
can be a "this." One man cannot see
things as another sees them. One can
only know things through knowing one-
self. Therefore it is said, " 'That' comes
from 'this,' and 'this' comes from 'that' "
—which means "that" and "this"
give birth to one another. Life arises
from death and death from life. What
is inappropriate is seen by virtue of
what is appropriate. There is right because of wrong, and wrong because of
right. Thus, the sage does not bother
with these distinctions but seeks enlight-
enment from heaven. So he sees "this,"
but "this" is also "that," and "that" is
also "this." "That" has elements of right
and wrong, and "this" has elements of
right and wrong. Does he still distinguish
between "this" and "that," or doesn't
he? When there is no more separation between "this" and "that," it is called the
still-point of Tao. At the still-point in
the center of the circle one can see the infinite in all things. Right is infinite; wrong
is also infinite. Therefore it is said, "Be-
hold the light beyond right and wrong."

To use one's fingers to demonstrate fingers not being fingers is not as good as using something else to demonstrate fingers not being fingers. Using horses to demonstrate horses not being horses is not as good as using something else to demonstrate horses not being horses. "Heaven and earth" are like a finger; "the ten thousand things" are like a horse.

What is acceptable is acceptable; what is not acceptable is not acceptable. A path is formed by walking on it. A thing has a name because of its being called something. Why is it like this? Because it is! Why is it not like that? Because it is not! Everything has its own nature and its own function. Nothing is without nature or function. Consider a small stalk or a great column, a leper or a beauty, things that are great or wicked, perverse, and strange. They are all one in Tao.

When there is separation, there is coming together. When there is coming together, there is dissolution. All things may become one, whatever their state of being. Only he who has transcended sees this oneness. He has no use for differences and dwells in the constant. To be constant is to be useful. To be useful is to realize one's true nature. Realization of one's true nature is happiness. When one reaches happiness, one is close to perfection. So one stops, yet does not know that one stops. This is Tao.

When you wrack your brain trying to unify things without knowing that they are already one, it is called "three in the morning." What do I mean by "three in the morning"? A man who kept monkeys said to them, "You get three acorns in the morning and four in the evening." This made them all very angry. So he said, "How about four in the morning and three in the evening?"—and the monkeys were happy. The number of acorns was the same, but the different arrangement resulted in anger or pleasure. This is what I am talking about. Therefore, the sage harmonizes right with wrong and rests in the balance of nature. This is called taking both sides at once.

以指喻指之非指不若以非指喻指之非指也
以馬喻馬之非馬不若以非馬喻馬之非馬也
天地一指也萬物一馬也可乎可不可乎不可
道行之而成
物謂之而然惡乎然然於然惡乎不然
不然於不然物固有所然物固有所可
無物不然無物不可故為是舉莛與楹
厲與西施恢恑憰怪道通為一
其分也成也其成也毀也凡物無成與毀復通為一
唯達者知通為一為是不用而寓諸庸
庸也者用也用也者通也通也者得也適得而幾已
因是已已而不知其然謂之道勞神明為一而不知其同也謂之朝三何謂朝三
狙公賦芧曰朝三而暮四眾狙皆怒曰然則朝四而暮三眾狙皆悅
名實未虧而喜怒為用亦因是也是以聖人和之以是非
而休乎天鈞是之謂兩行

Among the ancients, knowledge was very deep. What is meant by deep? It reached back to the time when nothing existed. It was so deep, so complete, that nothing could be added to it. Then came men who distinguished between things but did not give them names. Later they labeled them but did not choose between right and wrong. When right and wrong appeared, Tao declined. With the fall of Tao, desire arose. Is there really rise and fall?

When there is rise and fall, Chao Wen plays the lute. When there is no rise and fall, Chao Wen does not play the lute.

Chao Wen played the lute, Shia Kuang kept time with a baton, and Hui Tsu leaned on a stump and debated. Each of these three masters was nearly perfect in his own art. Their names will be remembered forevermore. Because they excelled, they were distinguished from others. Because they excelled, they wanted to enlighten others through their art. They tried to teach what could not be taught. This resulted in obscure discussions as to the nature of "hardness" and "whiteness." Their sons followed in their fathers' footsteps all their lives but accomplished nothing. However, if this can be called accomplishment, then even I have accomplished something. If this cannot be called accomplishment, then neither I nor others have accomplished anything. Therefore, the sage seeks insight from chaos and doubt. Not making distinctions but dwelling on that which is unchanging is called clear vision.

古之人其知有所至矣惡乎至
有以為未始有物者至矣盡矣
不可以加矣其次以為有物矣
而未始有封也其次以為有封焉
而未始有是非也是非之彰也
道之所以虧也道之所以虧
愛之所以成果且有成與虧乎哉
果且無成與虧乎哉
有成與虧故昭氏之鼓琴也
無成與虧故昭氏之不鼓琴也昭文之鼓琴也師曠之枝策也
惠子之據梧也三子之知幾乎皆其盛者也故載之末年唯其好之
也以異於彼其好之也欲以明之彼非所明而明之故以堅白之昧終
而其子又以文之綸終終身無成若是而可謂成乎
雖我亦成也若是而不可謂成乎物與我無成也
是故滑疑之耀聖人之所圖也為是不用而寓諸庸
此之謂以明

今且有言於此、不知其與是類乎、其與不是類乎、類與不類、相與為類、則與彼無以異矣、雖然、請嘗言之、有始也者、有未始有始也者、有未始有夫未始有始也者、有有也者、有無也者、有未始有無也者、有未始有夫未始有無也者、俄而有無矣、而未知有無之果孰有孰無也、今我則已有謂矣、而未知吾所謂之其果有謂乎、其果無謂乎、天下莫大於秋豪之末、而大山為小、莫壽於殤子、而彭祖為夭、天地與我並生、而萬物與我為一、既已為一矣、且得有言乎、既已謂之一矣、且得無言乎、一與言為二、二與一為三、自此以往、巧歷不能得、而況其凡乎、故自無適有以至於三、而況自有適有乎、無適焉、因是已

Now I am going to tell you something. I don't know what heading it comes under, and whether or not it is relevant here, but it must be relevant at some point. It is not anything new, but I would like to say it.

There is a beginning. There is no beginning of that beginning. There is no beginning of that no beginning of beginning. There is something. There is nothing. There is something before the beginning of something and nothing, and something before that. Suddenly there is something and nothing. But between something and nothing, I still don't really know which is something and which is nothing. Now, I've just said something, but I don't really know whether I've said anything or not.

There is nothing in the world greater than the tip of a bird's feather, and Mount Tai is small. None have lived longer than a dead child, and old Peng Tsu died young. Heaven and earth grow together with me, and the ten thousand things and I are one. We are already one—what else is there to say? Yet I have just said that we are one, so my words exist also. The one and what I said about the one make two, and two and one make three. Thus it goes on and on. Even a skilled mathematician cannot reach the end, much less an ordinary man. If we proceed from nothing to something, we reach three. How much farther would it be going from something to something? Enough. Let us stop.

夫道未始有封言未始有常為是而有畛也請言其畛有左有倫有義有分有辯有競有爭此之謂八德六合之外聖人存而不論六合之內聖人論而不議春秋經世先王之志聖人議而不辯故分也者有不分也辯也者有不辯也曰何也聖人懷之眾人辯之以相示也故曰辯也者有不見也

At first Tao had no name. Words are not eternal. Because of words, there are distinctions. Let me describe these distinctions. There is left, and there is right; there is relationship, and there is duty; there is discernment, and there is discrimination; there is competition, and there is struggle. These are called the eight virtues.

Beyond the six realms of heaven, earth, and the four directions, the sage accepts but does not discuss. Within the six realms, he discusses but does not pass judgment. In the Book of Spring and Autumn, the chronicle of the ancient kings, the sage passes judgment but does not question. When there is division, there is something which is not divided. When there is questioning, there is something beyond the question. Why is this? The sage keeps his wisdom to himself while ordinary men flaunt their knowledge in loud discussion. So I say, "Those who dispute do not see."

Great Tao is beyond description. Great argument uses no words. Great goodness is not kind. Great integrity is not incorruptible. Great courage is not aggressive. Tao that is manifest is not Tao. Words that argue miss the point. Perpetual kindness does not work. Obvious integrity is not believed. Aggressive courage will not win. These five are round and mellow, yet they may become square and inflexible.

Knowing enough to stop when one does not know is perfection.

Who can understand an argument that has no words and Tao that cannot be expressed? If a man can understand this, then he may be called the treasure house of heaven. Pour into it, and it will never be filled; pour out of it, and it will never be emptied. Yet no one knows why this is so. This is called the hidden light.

Long ago, Emperor Yao said to Shun, "I would like to attack the states of Tsung, Kuei, and Hsu Ao. This has been on my mind ever since I came to the throne. Why is this so?"

Shun said, "These three states eke out their existence in the weeds and bushes. Why bother? There was a time when ten suns rose all at once and the ten thousand things were illuminated. And yet how much greater is virtue than these suns!"

夫大道不稱，大辯不言，大仁不仁，大廉不嗛，大勇不忮。道昭而不道，言辯而不及，仁常而不成，廉清而不信，勇忮而不成。五者园而幾向方矣。故知止其所不知，至矣。孰知不言之辯，不道之道？若有能知，此之謂天府。注焉而不滿，酌焉而不竭，而不知其所由來，此之謂葆光。

故昔者堯問於舜曰：我欲伐宗、膾、胥敖，南面而不釋然。其故何也？舜曰：夫三子者，猶存乎蓬艾之間。若不釋然，何哉？昔者十日並出，萬物皆照，而況德之進乎日者乎！

Yeh Chueh asked Wang I, "Do you know what is common to all things?"

"How should I know?" he replied.

"Do you know that you don't know?"

"How should I know?" he replied again.

"Then are all things not knowable?"

"How should I know? Still, let me put it this way: How do you know that what I say I know may not really be what I don't know? How do you know that what I say I don't know may not really be what I know? Now let me ask you something. If a man sleeps in a damp place, his back will ache and he will be half paralyzed. But does this happen to eels? If a man lives up in a tree, he will tremble with fright. But does this happen to monkeys? Of these three, who knows the right place to live? Men eat flesh, deer eat grass, centipedes delight in worms, and owls and crows like mice. Of these four, which know what to eat? Monkeys mate with monkeys. Elk and deer run together, and eels play with fish.

"Mao Chiang and Li Chi were considered beautiful by men. But if fish saw them, they would dive to the bottom of the river. If birds saw them, they would fly off. If deer saw them, they would run away. Of these four, who recognizes real beauty?

"As I see it, the rules of goodness and wisdom and the paths of right and wrong are inextricably mingled and confused. How can I tell which is which?"

Yeh Chueh asked, "If you cannot distinguish between good and evil, then can the perfect man distinguish between them?"

Wang I replied, "The perfect man is spiritual. Though the great swamp burns, he will not feel the heat. Though the great rivers freeze, he will not feel the cold. Though thunderbolts split the mountains and gales shake the sea, he will have no fear. Such a man can ride the clouds and mist, mount the sun and moon, and wander beyond the four seas. Life and death do not affect him. How much less will he be concerned with good and evil!"

齧缺問乎王倪曰子知物之所同是乎曰吾惡乎知之
子知子之所不知邪曰吾惡乎知之然則物無知邪
曰吾惡乎知之雖然嘗試言之庸詎知吾所謂知之非不知邪
庸詎知吾所謂不知之非知邪且吾嘗試問乎女民溼寢則腰疾偏死
鰌然乎哉木處則惴慄恂懼猨猴然乎哉三者孰知正處
民食芻豢麋鹿食薦蝍且甘帶鴟鴉耆鼠四者孰知正味
猨猵狙以為雌麋與鹿交鰌與魚游毛嬙麗姬人之所美也
魚見之深入鳥見之高飛麋鹿見之決驟
四者孰知天下之正色哉自我觀之仁義之端是非之塗
樊然殽亂吾惡能知其辯齧缺曰子不知利害
則至人固不知利害乎王倪曰至人神矣
大澤焚而不能熱河漢沍而不能寒疾雷破山風振海
而不能驚若然者乘雲氣騎日月而遊乎四海之外
死生無變於己而況利害之端乎

Chu Chiao Tsu asked Chang Wu Tsu, "I have heard from Confucius that the sage is not troubled by worldly things. He does not look for gain or try to avoid loss; he seeks nothing, and does not cling to Tao. Sometimes he says something without words, and sometimes his words say nothing. Thus he travels beyond the dusty world. Confucius thought these words to be mere fantasy. But I think this is the way of the unfathomable Tao. What do you think?"

Chang Wu Tsu replied, "These words would have confused even the Yellow Emperor, so how could Confucius understand them? Moreover, you are too quick to draw conclusions. You see an egg, and immediately you listen for the crowing of a full-grown cock. You see a bow, and you look for a roast dove. Let me give you a rough explanation, but don't take this too literally. All right? How could anyone take his place beside the sun and moon, embrace the universe, be at one with all, refrain from interfering, and disregard the social order? Ordinary men labor and toil. The sage acts without choosing. He experiences ten thousand years as one age. To him the ten thousand things are what they are, yet they form a whole."

瞿鵲子問於長梧子曰夫子
望人不活るす方不就利不違害不喜求
不緣道天路有謂有謂天路
而遊墻之外夫子以るヒ孟浪之言而
我以为妙逍之引やる々るよ以る四め舍と苦
よ得よ日そ苗み命之所时炊焼やや
而已や何ヒ以免之見也か古計
見師而求时梧之欠禅而求鳩多次
予當为る女を之世忘妄听之
菜魯芳日月挟宇宙る天脇今
眾人役れ役塞人愚名第
置そ清睿以隷ね子
を引尸昂而一师绌
万物ハ也そ兆而朋星和理

予惡乎知説生之非惑邪　予惡乎知惡死之非弱喪而不知歸者邪

麗之姫艾封人之子也　晉國之始得之也　涕泣沾襟　及其至於王所　與王同筐床　食芻豢　而後悔其泣也

予惡乎知夫死者不悔其始之蘄生乎

夢飲酒者　旦而哭泣　夢哭泣者　旦而田獵　方其夢也　不知其夢也

夢之中又占其夢焉　覺而後知其夢也

且有大覺而後知此其大夢也

而愚者自以為覺　竊竊然知之

君乎　牧乎　固哉

丘也與女　皆夢也　予謂女夢　亦夢也

是其言也　其名為弔詭

萬世之後而一遇大聖　知其解者　是旦暮遇之也

"How can I tell if love of life is not a delusion? How can I tell whether a man who fears death is not like a man who has left home and dreads returning? Lady Li was the daughter of a border guard of Ai. When the Duke of Chin first took her captive, she wept until her dress was soaked with tears. But once she was living in the Duke's palace, sharing his bed, and eating delicious food, she wondered why she had ever cried. How can I tell whether the dead are not amazed that they ever clung to life?

"Those who dream of a great feast may weep the next morning. Those who dream of weeping may enjoy the hunt the next day. While they dream, they do not know they are dreaming. They may even interpret their dreams while still dreaming. Only after they awake do they know it was a dream. By and by, there will be a great awakening; then we will know that this is all a great dream. All the while, the fools think they are awake, appearing to understand things, calling this man ruler and that man herdsman. How stupid! You and Confucius are both dreaming. When I say you are dreaming, I am dreaming too. These words may sound like double-talk. Yet after ten thousand generations, we will meet a great sage who can explain all this. Or it may happen any time now."

Suppose you and I argue. If you win and I lose, are you indeed right and I wrong? And if I win and you lose, am I right and you wrong? Are we both partly right and partly wrong? Are we both all right or both all wrong? If you and I cannot see the truth, other people will find it even harder.

Then whom shall I ask to be the judge? Shall I ask someone who agrees with you? If he already agrees with you, how can he be a fair judge? Shall I ask someone who agrees with me? If he already agrees with me, how can he be a fair judge? Shall I ask someone who agrees with both of us? If he already agrees with both of us, how can he be a fair judge? Then if you and I and others cannot decide, shall we wait for still another? Waiting for changing opinions is like waiting for nothing. Seeing everything in relation to the heavenly cosmos and leaving the different viewpoints as they are, we may be able to live out our years.

What do I mean by seeing things in relation to the heavenly cosmos? Consider right and wrong, being and non-being. If right is indeed right, there need be no argument about how it is different from wrong. If being is really being, there need be no argument about how it is different from non-being. Forget time; forget distinction. Enjoy the infinite; rest in it.

既使我與若辯矣若勝我我不若勝若果是也
我果非也邪我勝若若不吾勝我果是也而果非也邪
其或是也其或非也邪其俱是也其俱非也邪
我與若不能相知也則人固受其黮闇吾誰使
正之使同乎若者正之既與若同矣惡能正之
使同乎我者正之既同乎我矣惡能正之
使異乎我與若者正之既異乎我與若矣惡能正之
使同乎我與若者正之既同乎我與若矣惡能正之
然則我與若與人俱不能相知也而待彼也邪
和之以天倪化聲之相待若其不相待和之以天
倪因之以曼衍所以窮年也
何謂和之以天倪曰是不是然不然是若果是也則
是之異乎不是也亦無辯
然若果然也則然之異乎不然也亦無辯
忘年忘義振於無竟故寓諸無竟

Shade said to Shadow, "A little while ago, you were moving; and now you are standing still. A little while ago, you were sitting down; and now you are getting up. Why all this indecision?"

Shadow replied, "Don't I have to depend on others to be what I am? Don't others also have to depend on something else to be what they are? My dependence is like that of the snake on his skin or of the cicada on his wings. How can I tell why I do this, or why I do that?"

Once upon a time, I, Chuang Tsu, dreamed I was a butterfly flying happily here and there, enjoying life without knowing who I was. Suddenly I woke up and I was indeed Chuang Tsu. Did Chuang Tsu dream he was a butterfly, or did the butterfly dream he was Chuang Tsu? There must be some distinction between Chuang Tsu and the butterfly. This is a case of transformation.

罔兩問景曰、曩子行今子止、曩子坐今子起、何其無特操與

景曰、吾有待而然者邪、吾所待又有待而然者邪、吾待蛇蚹蜩翼邪、惡識所以然、惡識所以不然

昔者莊周夢為胡蝶、栩栩然胡蝶也、自喻適志與、不知周也、俄然覺、則蘧蘧然周也、不知周之夢為胡蝶與、胡蝶之夢為周與、周與胡蝶則必有分矣、此之謂物化

CHAPTER THREE

THE SECRET
OF GROWTH

吾生也有涯而知也无涯
以有涯隨無涯殆巳
巳而知年殆而巳矣
為善无近名為惡无近刑
緣督以為經可以保身可以全生
可以养親可以尽年

Life has a limit, but knowledge is without limit. For the limited to pursue the unlimited is futile. To know this and still pursue knowledge is even more futile. In doing good, avoid fame. In doing evil, avoid punishment. Thus, by pursuing the middle way, you may preserve your body, fulfill your life, look after your parents, and live out your years.

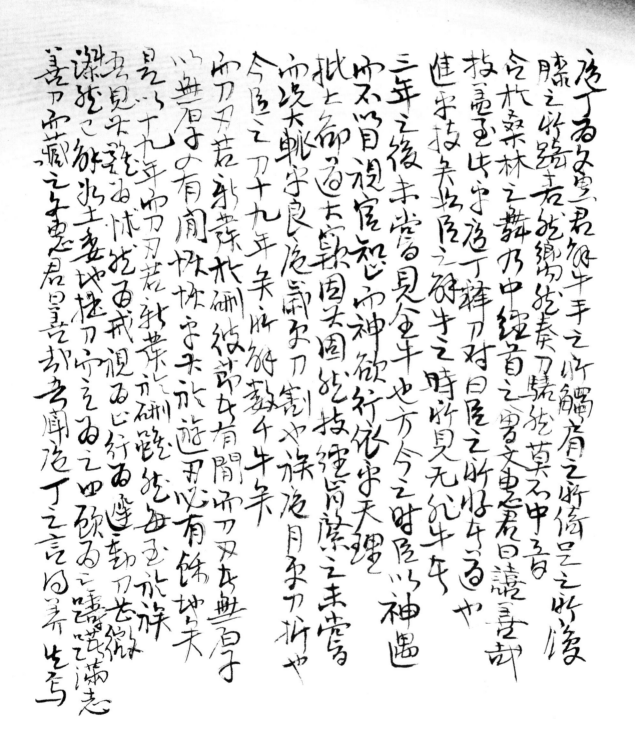

Prince Wen Hui's cook was carving up an ox. Every touch of his hand, every heave of his shoulder, every step of his foot, every thrust of his knee, with the slicing and parting of the flesh, and the zinging of the knife—all was in perfect rhythm, just like the Dance of the Mulberry Grove or a part in the Ching Shou symphony.

Prince Wen Hui remarked, "How wonderfully you have mastered your art."

The cook laid down his knife and said, "What your servant really cares for is Tao, which goes beyond mere art. When I first began to cut up oxen, I saw nothing but oxen. After three years of practicing, I no longer saw the ox as a whole. I now work with my spirit, not with my eyes. My senses stop functioning and my spirit takes over. I follow the natural grain, letting the knife find its way through the many hidden openings, taking advantage of what is there, never touching a ligament or tendon, much less a main joint.

"A good cook changes his knife once a year because he cuts, while a mediocre cook has to change his every month because he hacks. I've had this knife of mine for nineteen years and have cut up thousands of oxen with it, and yet the edge is as if it were fresh from the grindstone. There are spaces between the joints. The blade of the knife has no thickness. That which has no thickness has plenty of room to pass through these spaces. Therefore, after nineteen years, my blade is as sharp as ever. However, when I come to a difficulty, I size up the joint, look carefully, keep my eyes on what I am doing, and work slowly. Then with a very slight movement of the knife, I cut the whole ox wide open. It falls apart like a clod of earth crumbling to the ground. I stand there with the knife in my hand, looking about me with a feeling of accomplishment and delight. Then I wipe the knife clean and put it away."

"Well done!" said the Prince. "From the words of my cook, I have learned the secret of growth."

公ふ狩見右師霞鶯日是有人や悲来今心天与弓人与日天や死人や

天之先是依独や人之貌有与や以是至天天や死人や

準雉十牛一味る半一飲不斬音半樊中神る无不喜や

56

When Kung Wen Hsien saw the Commander of the Army, he was startled and exclaimed, "Who is this? Why does he have only one foot? Was it the work of heaven or of man?" The Commander said, "It was the work of heaven, not man. Heaven made me one-footed. Heaven determines man's appearance; therefore I know it was heaven, not man. The pheasant in the marshes has to take ten steps in order to get one beakful of food, one hundred steps for one drink of water. Yet it doesn't want to be kept in a cage. Though it would be fed like a king, it would not be happy."

When Lao Tsu died, Chin Shih went to the funeral. He yelled three times and left.

A disciple said, "Were you not a friend of the Master?"

"Yes."

"Then is it proper to mourn him in this way?"

"Yes. When I first arrived, I thought his spirit was really there. Now I know it wasn't. When I went in to mourn, the old people were wailing as though they had lost their son. The young ones were crying as though they had lost their mother. Since they were all together, they talked and wept without any control. This is avoiding heaven, indulging in sentiment, ignoring what is natural. In the old days, it was called the crime of violating the law of nature.

"The Master came because it was time. He left because he followed the natural flow. Be content with the moment, and be willing to follow the flow; then there will be no room for grief or joy. In the old days this was called freedom from bondage. The wood is consumed but the fire burns on, and we do not know when it will come to an end."

人間性

CHAPTER FOUR

HUMAN AFFAIRS

Yen Hui went to Confucius to say goodbye.

The Master asked, "Where are you going?"

"I am going to Wei."

"What are you going to do there?"

"I hear that the Prince of Wei is young and that he is arbitrary in his actions. He is not much concerned with his country and is not aware of his mistakes. He thinks nothing of people dying. The dead lie everywhere like thick grass in a swamp.

The people have nowhere to turn. I've heard you, Master, say, 'Leave the country that is already well governed and go to a country that is in chaos.' At the door of a physician, there are many sick people. I would like to use your teaching to remedy the situation there."

Confucius said, "Ah! If you go there, you will only get into trouble. Tao must be pure. When something is added to it, there is confusion. When there is confusion, there is anxiety. With anxiety, there is no hope. The wise men of old realized Tao in themselves before they offered it to others. If you are not certain that you have it in yourself, how can you change a tyrant's action?

"Besides, do you know how virtue degenerates and how learning arises? Virtue is consumed by fame. Learning is born of contention. Fame causes men to fight with one another. Learning is the weapon for the struggle. Both can be evil instruments. They are not the means to perfection. Though you are highly virtuous and trustworthy, if you do not understand the spirit of men, and though you are famous and do not compete, if you do not understand the minds of men, but instead go to a tyrant and lecture him on goodness, ethical behavior, measures and standards, you are just using the failings of others to demonstrate your own superiority. This is deliberately hurting other people. One who hurts others will in turn be hurt. You will probably end up in trouble."

顏回見仲尼請行曰奚之曰將之衛曰奚為焉其年壯其行獨
而不見其過輕用民死死者以國量乎澤若蕉民其無如矣回嘗聞之夫子曰治國去之
亂國就之醫門多疾願以所聞思其則庶幾其國有瘳乎仲尼曰譆若殆往而刑耳
夫道不欲雜雜則多多則擾擾則憂憂而不救古之至人先存諸己而後存諸人
所存於己者未定何暇至於暴人之所行且若亦知夫德之所蕩而知之所為出乎哉
德蕩乎名知出乎爭名也者相軋也知也者爭之器也二者凶器非所以盡行也
且德厚信矼未達人氣名聞不爭未達人心而彊以仁義繩墨之言術暴人之前者
是以人惡有其美也命之曰菑人菑人者人必反菑之若殆為人菑夫

"If indeed the Prince likes good men and hates bad men, why would you try to change him? If he does not, you would be better off saying nothing; for if you do speak, the Prince will expose your weak points and win the argument. You will look confused and ashamed; you will find one excuse after another and you will seem to yield. Your mind will be molded to his way of thinking. This is putting out fire with fire, adding water to a flood; it is called adding to the excess. If you start by giving in, there will be no end to your concessions. And if you speak out strongly against him, he will not listen to you and will undoubtedly put you to death.

"In ancient times, Chieh killed Kuan Lung Pang and Chou killed Prince Pi Kan. These two victims were virtuous men who tried hard to comfort and aid the common people. In this way they offended their superiors. Their rulers had them put to death because of their goodness. This was the result of seeking fame for their virtue. Many years ago, Yao attacked the states of Tsung Chi and Hsu Ao; Yu attacked Yuo Hu. These nations were laid waste and destroyed, their rulers killed. For all of them were constantly at war in an effort to win more. They were all seekers of fame and wealth. Have you never heard of them? Even wise men cannot deal with fame and wealth. So how can you? However, you must have something else in mind. Come tell me what it is."

顏回曰端而虛勉而一則可乎曰惡惡可夫以陽為充孔揚
采色不定常人之所不違因案人之所感以求容與其心名之曰
日漸之德不成而況大德乎將執而不化外合而內不訾其庸詎可乎
然則我內直而外曲成而上比內直者與天為徒
與天為徒者知天子之與己皆天之所子
而獨以己言蘄乎而人善之蘄乎而人不善之邪
若然者人謂之童子是之謂與天為徒
外曲者與人之為徒也擎跽曲拳
人臣之禮也人皆為之吾敢不為邪
為人之所為者人亦無疵焉是之謂與人為徒
成而上比者與古為徒其言雖教讁之實也
古之有也非吾有也若然者雖直而不病
是之謂與古為徒若是則可乎
仲尼曰惡惡可大多政法而不諜
雖固亦無罪雖然止是耳矣夫胡可以及化
猶師心者也

Yen Hui said, "If I am detached and self-assured, persevering and of one mind, won't that work?"

"What! How can that work? You may put on a brave show, but your uncertainty will appear on your face as it would with anyone else. This prince takes pleasure in exploiting the feelings of others. He cannot even practice the ordinary virtues. How do you expect him to appreciate the higher virtues? He will be obstinate and unbending. Outwardly he may agree, but there will be no inward change of heart. How can you succeed in that way?"

"Well then, I will be inwardly firm and outwardly compliant. I will arm myself with examples from antiquity. Being inwardly firm, I will be a follower of heaven. Being a follower of heaven, I know that the Prince and I are both sons of heaven. So, why should I mind whether or not people approve of my words? People call this being childlike. This is what I call being a follower of heaven.

"By being outwardly compliant, I am a follower of men. Lifting the tablet, kneeling, bending, and bowing—this is how a minister behaves. All men do this. Why shouldn't I? Do as others do, and there is no trouble! This is what I call being a follower of men.

"By observing the customs, I will be following ancient tradition. Though my words may be chiding and critical, they will not be my own words but the words of the sages. So I need not be afraid of speaking out. This is what I mean by following tradition. Will that work?"

Confucius said, "How could that work? You have too many plans. They are fine but not appropriate. These preconceived ideas probably won't get you into trouble, but that is as far as they go. How can you possibly influence him? You are still too rigid in your thinking."

Yen Hui said, "That is all I can think of. May I ask what to do?"

Confucius said, "You must fast. I'll tell you why. Is it easy to work from preconceived ideas? Heaven frowns on those who think it is easy."

Yen Hui said, "My family is poor. I have neither drunk wine nor eaten meat for many months. Can this be considered fasting?"

Confucius replied, "That is the fasting one does for sacrificial ceremonies, not the fasting of the mind."

Yen Hui said, "May I ask what is fasting of the mind?"

Confucius said, "Your will must be one. Do not listen with your ears but with your mind. Do not listen with your mind but with your vital energy. Ears can only hear, mind can only think, but vital energy is empty, receptive to all things. Tao abides in emptiness. Emptiness is the fasting of mind."

Yen Hui said, "Before I heard all this, I was certain that I was Hui. Now that I've heard it, I am no longer Hui. Can this be called emptiness?"

Confucius said, "That is it. Let me explain. You can enter this man's service, but do not thrust yourself forward. If he listens, then speak. If not, be silent. Leave no opening, and you will not be harmed. Be always at one and accept whatever happens. Then you are close to success. If you do not move, then it is easy to remain unnoticed. But it is hard to walk without touching the ground. It is easy to be a hypocrite in your dealings with men. It is hard to be a hypocrite in your dealings with heaven.

"You understand how to fly using wings, but you have not yet seen how to fly without them. You understand how to act from knowledge, but you have not yet seen how to act from not-knowing. Look at empty space. It is in emptiness that light is born. There is happiness in stillness. Lack of stillness is called sitting while wandering. If you are open to everything you see and hear, and allow this to act through you, even gods and spirits will come to you, not to speak of men. This is the transformation of the ten thousand things, the secret of the wise kings Yu and Shun, the constant practice of Fu Hsi and Chi Chu. It is even more useful for ordinary men."

顏回曰吾无以進矣敢問其方仲尼曰齋吾將語若
有而為之其易邪易之者暭天不宜顏回曰
回之家貧唯不飲酒不茹葷者數月矣如此
則可以為齋乎曰是祭祀之齋非心齋也
回曰敢問心齋仲尼曰若志无聽之以耳而聽
之以心无聽之以心而聽之以氣聽止於耳心止
於符氣也者虛而待物者也唯道集虛虛者心齋也
顏回曰回之未始得使實自回也得使之也未始有回
也可謂虛乎夫子曰盡矣吾語若若能入遊其樊
而无感其名入則鳴不入則止无門无毒一宅
而寓於不得已則幾矣絕迹易无行地難為人使
易以偽為天使難以偽聞以有翼飛者矣未聞以
无翼飛者也聞以有知知者矣未聞以无知知者也
瞻彼闋者虛室生白吉祥止止夫且不止是之謂
坐馳夫徇耳目內通而外於心知鬼神將來舍
而況人乎是萬物之化也禹舜之所紐也伏戲
几蘧之所行終而況散焉者乎

Tsu Kao, the Duke of She, was being sent to the state of Chi on a mission, and went first to consult Confucius, saying, "The King is dispatching me on a very important mission. Chi will probably treat me with great respect but will be slow to start our discussions. Even an ordinary man is not easily hurried, much less a feudal lord. I am very worried. You always said to me, 'In all matters, great or small, few will succeed without following Tao.' If this mission is not successful, I shall be criticized. If it is successful, I will be troubled by confusion and anxiety. Only a wise man is not concerned with results—and is therefore unaffected by the outcome. I eat simple unspiced food, so I never need cooling drinks. I received these orders one morning, and by the evening I was drinking vast quantities of water. Am I not feverish? I have not yet seen the actual situation and already I am troubled by anxiety and confusion. If I do not succeed, I am bound to be criticized. I am in a double bind. This is beyond my capacity as a minister. Will you tell me what to do?"

葉子高將使於齊問於仲尼曰王使
之夫猶未可動而況諸侯乎吾甚慄
實不道以懽成了若不成則必有人道之患
若不成則而後先患去唯有德者能之
今吾朝受命而夕飲冰我其內熱與
子若不至乎有人道之患是兩也

諸梁也甚重齊之待使者蓋將甚敬而不急
之子常語諸梁也曰凡事若小若大
若成則必有陰陽之患事若
爨無欲清之人居未知吾
兩也為人臣者不足以任之子其有以語我來

Confucius replied, "In the affairs of the world, two universal principles may be observed: one is the natural order and the other is duty. It is natural for a son to love his parents; this cannot be erased from his heart. It is duty for a man to serve his sovereign; everywhere he goes there will be a sovereign. Within heaven and earth, there is no escape. That is why they are called universal principles. Therefore, to honor one's parents, wherever one may be, is the fullness of devotion. To serve one's sovereign willingly, whatever happens, is the perfect loyalty. To serve one's own mind, unmoved by sadness or joy, accepting whatever happens, is the true virtue. Being a son or a subject, there is always something unavoidable that one has to do. Do what has to be done and give no thought to yourself; then you will not have time to think about loving life and hating death. Continue in this way and all will go well.

"Let me tell you something else I have heard. If states have close ties, their mutual trust is demonstrated by deeds. If they are far apart, their good faith has to be renewed with words in the form of messages. But carrying messages of delight or anger between two parties is the most difficult thing in the world. When they are both pleased, there is bound to be exaggeration of flattery; when they are both angry, there is bound to be exaggeration of criticism. Exaggeration leads away from truth. Without truth, there will be no trust. When there is no trust, the messengers will be in danger. Therefore, it is said, 'Speak the truth and do not exaggerate; then you will not be harmed.'"

"Moreover, when wrestlers pit their strength against each other, they begin in a lighthearted, open frame of mind but they usually end up looking angry. At the height of the contest, many crafty tricks are played. When men drink during ceremonies, they start off in an orderly manner and usually finish in disarray. At the height of the party, fun becomes chaos. So it is with all things. They begin in good faith and end up in meanness. What was simple in the beginning becomes grotesque in the end. Words are like the wind and the waves; action involves the risk of gain or loss. The wind and the waves are easily set in motion; risk can easily turn into real danger. Hence, anger comes from nothing more than clever words and half-truths. When animals face death, they do not care what noises they make. They growl fiercely and snarl, and then they attack. In the same way, if a man is pushed too far, he turns and strikes without knowing why. If he does not know why, who knows where it will lead? Therefore, it is said, 'Neither deviate from your instructions, nor hurry to finish.' Do not force things. It is dangerous to deviate from instructions or push for completion. It takes a long time to do a thing properly. Once you do something wrong, it may be too late to change it. Can you afford to be careless?

"So then, flow with whatever may happen and let your mind be free; stay centered by accepting whatever you are doing. This is the ultimate. How else can you carry out your task? It is best to leave everything to work naturally, though this is not easy."

且以勇鬪力を持す陽常卒中陰大玉刻多才を
以れ飲泣此將に常卒中乱大玉刻多与未凡る点也
將中泳常卒中品夫作將や簡夫將畢や必臣夫言也
凧波や行衣實喪や凧波烏以動實喪別以り己
なを怠没無由云言偏辭獣氣不揮音氣息非也
知是爰先心屬刻核大玉則必有不束前忘死也
苟万石知云死や熱を知死死をめ知云死や
過度云玉や遣今功別強ら善則左久
悪別不及波むこ塊て也
墨来乗物以遊心沿ゐ見心毒や申
玉兵何作因披又其若石波合命
半云难年

顏闔將傅衛靈公太子而問於蘧伯玉曰
有人於此其德天殺與之為無方則危吾國
與之為有方則危吾身其知適足以知人之過
而不知其所以過若然者吾奈之何
蘧伯玉曰善哉問乎戒之慎之正汝身也哉
形莫若就心莫若和雖然之二者有患
就不欲入和不欲出形就而入且為顛為滅
為崩為蹶心和而出且為聲為名
為妖為孽
彼且為嬰兒亦與之為嬰兒
彼且為無町畦亦與之為無町畦
彼且為無崖亦與之為無崖
達之入於無疵

Yen Ho was about to become tutor of the Crown Prince, the son of Duke Ling of the state of Wei. He went to consult Chu Po Yu, saying, "Here is someone who is naturally violent. If I let him remain undisciplined, the state will be in danger. If I try to correct him, I shall endanger myself. He knows enough to see the faults of others, but not to see his own. Under these circumstances, what shall I do?"

Chu Po Yu replied, "That is a good question! Be on guard, be careful, and be sure that you yourself are acting appropriately. Appear to be flexible but maintain harmony within. However, there is danger in doing these two things. While being flexible, be sure to remain centered.

While maintaining harmony within, do not display it openly. If you are too flexible and lose your center, then you will be overcome and destroyed, and you will collapse. If you try to demonstrate your composure, you will be criticized and slandered, called a devil and a son of a bitch. If he wants to be a child, be a child with him. If he wants to act strangely, act strangely with him. If he wants to be reckless, be reckless with him. Then you can reach him and bring him back to his senses."

"Do you know the story of the praying mantis? It raised its arm to stop an approaching carriage unaware that this was beyond its power. Such was its high opinion of itself. Watch out and be careful. If you offend the Prince by showing off your own talents, you court disaster.

"Do you know how a tiger trainer works? He does not risk feeding the tigers live animals for fear of arousing their ferocity as they kill. He does not risk feeding them whole animals for fear of arousing their anger as they tear them apart. He knows when the tigers are hungry and when they are full; thereby he is in touch with their fierce nature. Tigers are a different species from men, yet by observing their ways, one can train them to be gentle. They will kill only when aroused.

"A man with a passion for horses catches the manure in a basket and the piss in a jar. If a mosquito or a fly lands on the horse and he brushes it off too abruptly, then the horse will break its bit, hurt the man's head, and crack his ribs. Such a man has good intentions, but he overdoes it. Can you afford to be careless?"

汝不知夫螳螂乎怒其臂以當車轍不知其不勝任也是其才之美者也

戒之慎之積伐而美者以犯之幾矣

汝不知夫養虎者乎不敢以生物與之為其

殺之之怒也不敢以全物與之

為其決之之怒也時其飢飽達其怒心虎之與人異類而媚養己者順也

故其殺者逆也

夫愛馬者以筐盛矢以蜄盛溺適有蚉虻僕緣而拊之不時則缺

銜毀首碎胸

意有所至而愛有所亡可不慎邪

Shih the carpenter was on his way to the state of Chi. When he got to Chu Yuan, he saw an oak tree by the village shrine. The tree was large enough to shade several thousand oxen and was a hundred spans around. It towered above the hilltops with its lowest branches eighty feet from the ground. More than ten of its branches were big enough to be made into boats. There were crowds of people as in a marketplace. The master carpenter did not even turn his head but walked on without stopping.

His apprentice took a long look, then ran after Shih the carpenter and said, "Since I took up my ax and followed you, master, I have never seen timber as beautiful as this. But you do not even bother to look at it and walk on without stopping. Why is this?"

Shih the carpenter replied, "Stop! Say no more! That tree is useless. A boat made from it would sink, a coffin would soon rot, a tool would split, a door would ooze sap, and a beam would have termites. It is worthless timber and is of no use. That is why it has reached such a ripe old age."

匠石之齊至于曲轅
見櫟社樹其大蔽數千牛
絜之百圍其高臨山十仞而後有枝
其可以為舟者旁十數觀者如市
匠伯不顧遂行不輟
弟子厭觀之走及匠石曰
自吾執斧斤以隨夫子未嘗見材如此其美也
先生不肯視行不輟何邪
曰已矣勿言之矣散木也以為舟則沈
以為棺椁則速腐
以為器則速毀以為門戸則液樠
以為柱則蠹是不材之木也

After Shih the carpenter had returned home, the sacred oak appeared to him in a dream, saying, "What are you comparing me with? Are you comparing me with useful trees? There are cherry, apple, pear, orange, citron, pomelo, and other fruit trees. As soon as the fruit is ripe, the trees are stripped and abused. Their large branches are split, and the smaller ones torn off. Their life is bitter because of their usefulness. That is why they do not live out their natural lives but are cut off in their prime. They attract the attentions of the common world. This is so for all things. As for me, I have been trying for a long time to be useless. I was almost destroyed several times. Finally I am useless, and this is very useful to me. If I had been useful, could I have ever grown so large?

"Besides, you and I are both things. How can one thing judge another thing? What does a dying and worthless man like you know about a worthless tree?" Shih the carpenter awoke and tried to understand his dream.

His apprentice said, "If it had so great a desire to be useless, why does it serve as a shrine?"

Shih the carpenter said, "Hush! Stop talking! It is just pretending to be one so that it will not be hurt by those who do not know it is useless. If it had not become a sacred tree, it would probably have been cut down. It protects itself in a different way from ordinary things. We will miss the point if we judge it in the ordinary way."

匠石曰櫟社見夢曰
女將惡乎比予哉若將比予於文木耶
夫柤梨橘柚果蓏之屬實熟則剝
剝則辱大枝折小枝泄
此以其能苦其生者也
故不終其天年而中道夭
自掊擊於世俗者也物莫不若是
且予求無所可用久矣幾死乃今得之為予大用
使予也而有用且得有此大也耶
且也若與予皆物也奈何哉其相物也
而幾死之散人又惡知散木
匠石覺而診其夢弟子曰趣取無用則為社何耶
曰密若無言彼亦直寄焉以為不知己者
詬厲也不為社者且幾有翦乎

Nan Po Tsu Chi was wandering in the Shang Hills when he caught sight of a huge, extraordinary tree. A thousand four-horse chariots could have rested in its shade. Tsu Chi said, "What kind of tree is this? It must be very special wood." He looked up and saw that the smaller branches were gnarled and twisted, and could not be used for beams or rafters. He looked down and saw that the great trunk was curved and knotted, and could not be used for coffins. When he tasted a leaf, it burned his mouth; when he sniffed it, he became intoxicated and for three days acted as if he were drunk. Tsu Chi said, "Indeed, this tree is good for nothing. No wonder it grew so big. That is how it is! Holy men treasure this worthlessness."

Ching Shih in the province of Sung is a good place for growing catalpa, cypress, and mulberry trees. Those trees that attain the girth of a span or more are cut down to make monkey perches. Those of three or four spans are cut down to make beams for tall, elegant houses. Those of seven or eight spans are cut down to make side boards for the coffins of aristocratic and rich merchant families.

So, these trees never achieve their full stature but fall in their prime under the blows of the ax. Such are the hazards of being useful.

In the same way, oxen with white foreheads, pigs with turned-up snouts, and men with piles may not be sacrificed to the River God. Shamans believe these creatures bring bad luck. Holy men, however, believe they are very fortunate.

南伯子綦遊乎商之丘見大木焉有異結駟千乘
隱將芘其所藾子綦曰此何木也哉此必有異材夫
仰而視其細枝則拳曲而不可以為棟樑俯而視其大根
則軸解而不可以為棺槨咶其葉則口爛而為傷
嗅之則使人狂酲三日而不已子綦曰此果不材之木也
以至於此其大也嗟乎神人以此不材
宋有荊氏者宜楸柏桑其拱把而上者求狙猴之杙者斬之
三圍四圍求高名之麗者斬之七圍八圍貴人富商之家
求樿傍者斬之故未終其天年而中道之夭於斧斤
此材之患也故解之以牛之白顙者與豚之亢鼻者
與人有痔病者不可以適河此皆巫祝以知之矣
所以為不祥也此乃神人之所以為大祥也

支離疏者頤隱於臍肩高於頂會撮指天五管在上兩髀為脅
挫鍼治繲足以餬口鼓筴播精足以食十人上徵武士
則支離攘臂而遊於其間上有大役
則支離以有常疾不受功
上與病者粟則受三鐘與十束薪
夫支離其形者
猶足以養其身
終其天年
又況支離其德者乎

There was once a hunchback called Shu. His chin rested on his navel, his shoulders rose up over his head, and his neck bone pointed to the sky. His five vital organs were upside down, and his hips were level with his ribs. By sewing and taking in laundry, he made enough to feed himself. By winnowing and sifting grain, he earned enough to support ten people. When the authorities were raising an army, he came and went without having to hide. When a big public project was planned, he was assigned no work because he was a chronic invalid. When the government was giving free grain to the sick, he received three measures and ten bundles of firewood. If a man whose body is strange can take care of himself and live to the end of his natural life, how much easier it is for a man with strange behavior.

孔子商[楚]狂接輿遊並門曰鳳兮鳳兮
何如德之衰也求之石可待徒也乃子迂也
天下有之道聖人成爲天下無道聖人生爲
方今之時僅免刑爲福甄吏羽章之智載
渦彙平地莫之知避己乎之平臨人以德
始乎治乎書地而趨速隍速隍
元傷吾行吾行郤曲元傷吾足
山木自寇也膏火自煎也
桂可食故伐之漆可用故割之
人皆知有用之用而莫知元用之用也

When Confucius was in the state of Chu, the madman of Chu, Chieh Yu, stood at his gate and cried, "O phoenix, O phoenix, how virtue has declined! One cannot wait for the future. One cannot chase after the past. When Tao is in the world, the sage achieves perfection; when Tao is absent, the sage merely bides his time. In times like these the best you can do is to stay out of trouble. Happiness is as light as a feather, but nobody knows how to bear it. Calamity is as heavy as the earth, but nobody knows how to avoid it. Enough! Enough of this confronting people with virtue! Beware! Beware of trudging down this marked path. Oh, thorns, thorns! You do not block my way. My path twists around you. You do not hurt my feet.

"The mountain trees ask to be chopped down. Fat added to the fire consumes itself. The cinnamon tree is edible, so it is cut down. The lacquer tree is useful, so it is slashed. Everyone knows the usefulness of the useful, but no one knows the usefulness of the useless."

CHAPTER FIVE

SIGNS OF
FULL VIRTUE

魯有兀者王駘從之遊者與仲尼相若常季問於仲尼曰王駘
兀者也從之遊者與夫子中分魯立不教坐不議虛而往
實而歸固有不言之教無形而心成者邪是何人也
仲尼曰夫子聖人也丘也直後而未往耳丘將以為師
而況不若丘者乎奚假魯國丘將引天下而與從之
常季曰彼兀者也而王先生
其與庸亦遠矣若然者
其用心也獨若之何仲尼曰
死生亦大矣而不得與之變
雖天地覆墜亦將不與之遺
審乎無假而不與物遷
命物之化而守其宗也常季曰
何謂也仲尼曰自其異者視之
肝膽楚越也自其同者視之萬物皆一也
夫若然者且不知耳目之所宜而游心乎德之和
物視其所一而不見其所喪
視喪其足猶遺土也

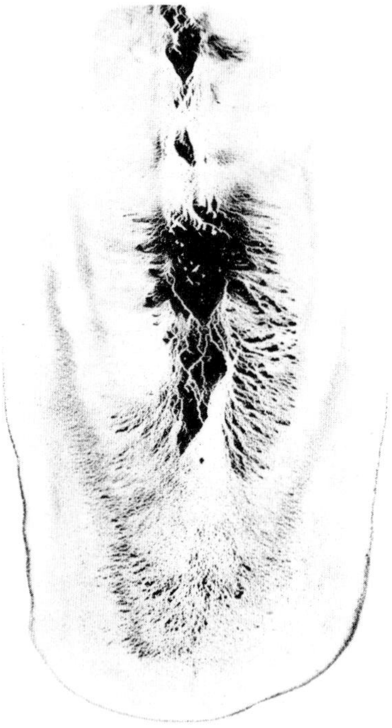

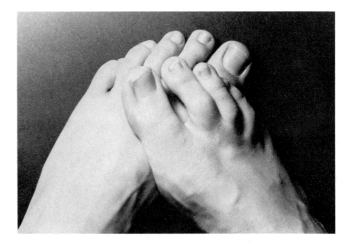

In the state of Lu, there was a man named Wang Tai who had but one foot. He had as many followers as Confucius. Chang Chi asked Confucius, "This Wang Tai is a cripple, yet he has as many followers in the state of Lu as you do. When he stands up, he does not teach. When he sits down, he utters no word. People go to him empty, and come back full. Is there such a thing as teaching without words? Can the mind be perfect while the body is deformed? What kind of man is he?"

Confucius said, "This man is a sage. It is just that I have been a little slow in going to see him. I myself am going to make him my teacher. Why shouldn't all of you who are my disciples do the same? I shall bring the whole world, not just the state of Lu, to sit at his feet."

Chang Chi said, "He is a cripple, yet he can be your teacher. He must be quite an extraordinary man. What is unique about the way he uses his mind?"

Confucius said, "Death and life are important, yet they do not affect him. Heaven and earth may collapse, yet he remains unmoved. He perceives the true reality and is not affected by external appearances. He lets things change naturally, and so he holds fast to the roots."

Chang Chi said, "What do you mean?"

Confucius said, "If we observe things from the point of view of their differences, liver and gall are as unlike one another as the state of Chu in the west and the state of Yueh in the east. If we see that which is the same in all things, then the ten thousand things are one. He who sees things in this light is not distracted by what reaches him through his ears and his eyes but lets his mind follow the natural harmony. He sees all things as one and is not troubled by loss. To him, the loss of his foot is just like throwing away so much dirt."

常不自得るも哎を知る志以志心日去常心
物困る是敢之部仲伲色人草贈打居吹
而贈打己北吃心此独已思以学命栌坤
隹打柏独や在冬多青青学命折天
唯舞独や止幸独止幸心已思生
夫保此之後羅之寄角七人雄守九年
将扎礼石卉自安女究独若牛
雲沉宣天地祥乃为物宝寅之競
家子月一瓶之好色応心丰喜死右宇
彼見拝日宫拴傺人魚隂生や
彼見何旨以称る了宇

Chang Chi said, "He is for himself. He uses his knowledge to perfect his mind and he uses his mind to attain the universal mind. Why do people turn to him in such numbers?"

Confucius said, "Men cannot see their reflection in running water but only in still water. Only that which is still in itself can still the seekers of stillness. Of those things that receive life from the earth, the pine and cypress trees alone stand out. They remain green summer and winter long. Of those that receive life from heaven, the wise King Shun alone was upright. Being fortunate, he was able to order his own life and thus order the lives of others. Holding fast to one's own roots is the foundation of courage. A single brave soldier may overcome nine armies. If he can do this simply because he wants recognition, how much more can be done by one who rules heaven and earth, who embraces the ten thousand things, who dwells only for a time in the body, whose ears and eyes are just for forming images, who unifies all knowledge and never experiences death? He will soon, at a time of his own choosing, leave the dusty world and rise to another level. The world will naturally follow him. Why should he be concerned with the affairs of the world?"

Shen Tu Chia had had his foot cut off as punishment. He and Tsu Chan, the Prime Minister of the state of Cheng, were students of Po Hun Wu Jen.

Tsu Chan said to Shen Tu Chia, "If I leave first, you will stay behind. If you leave first, I will stay behind."

The next day they were once more sitting together in the hall on the same mat. Tsu Chan said to Shen Tu Chia, "If I leave first, you will stay behind. If you leave first, I will stay behind. Now that I am about to leave, will you stay behind or not? I might add that when you see me, you do not even move out of the way. Perhaps you think that you are the equal of a Prime Minister?"

Shen Tu Chia said, "In our master's house is there such a thing as a Prime Minister? Perhaps you are proud of being a Prime Minister and being above everybody. I have heard that if a mirror is bright, dust and dirt will not settle on it. If they do, then it is not really bright. If one remains with a wise man for a long time, one will be without faults. Now, you are seeking great things from our master, yet you still talk like this. Is this proper?"

Tsu Chan said, "Take a look at yourself! You still think that you can be as good as Yao. Examine your virtues. Perhaps you will have cause to reflect."

Shen Tu Chia said, "Those who justify their faults to avoid punishment are many, and those who do not justify their faults and refuse to be spared are few. But only the virtuous man can resign himself to the inevitable and accept it as fate. Those who wander in front of archer Yi's target will be hit. If they do not get hit, it is fate. Many people who have both feet laugh at me for having only one. I used to explode with anger. Since I came to study with the Master, I have changed completely. Perhaps he has washed me clean with his goodness. I have been with the Master for nineteen years, and I have never been aware of having only one foot. Now, you and I are supposed to be concerned with our inner selves and yet you pay attention to my external body. Is this proper?"

Tsu Chan was disconcerted, his expression changed, and he asked Shen Tu Chia to say no more.

申徒嘉兀者也而與鄭子產同師於伯昏無人
子產謂申徒嘉曰我先出則子止子先出則我止
其明日又與合堂同席而坐子產謂申徒嘉曰
我先出則子止子先出則我止今我將出子可以止乎
其未邪且子見執政而不違子齊執政乎
申徒嘉曰先生之門固有執政焉如此哉
子而說子之執政而後人者也
聞之曰鑑明則塵垢不止止則不明也
久與賢人處則無過今子之所取大者先生也
而猶出言若是不亦過乎

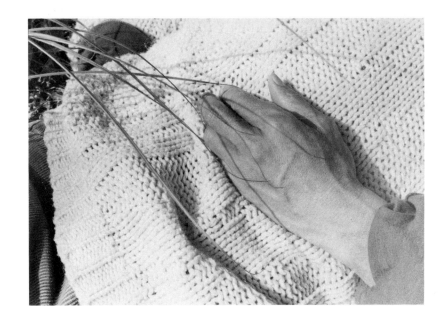

子産曰子皆若要吳猶身免是乎計其爲
申信嘉曰自狀吉南以石吉以在羽石狀云
及石而奉高安之若命悔有能年然之遊水
申東斗中怡や於石申年命や余失善亡笑
牡将金亦怨而高先生之然勿勝紀如及石
言善吉と辞之大平吳而子亲世子邦晗
寸産訛然路蒼冬子文乃
徐如羽石南市

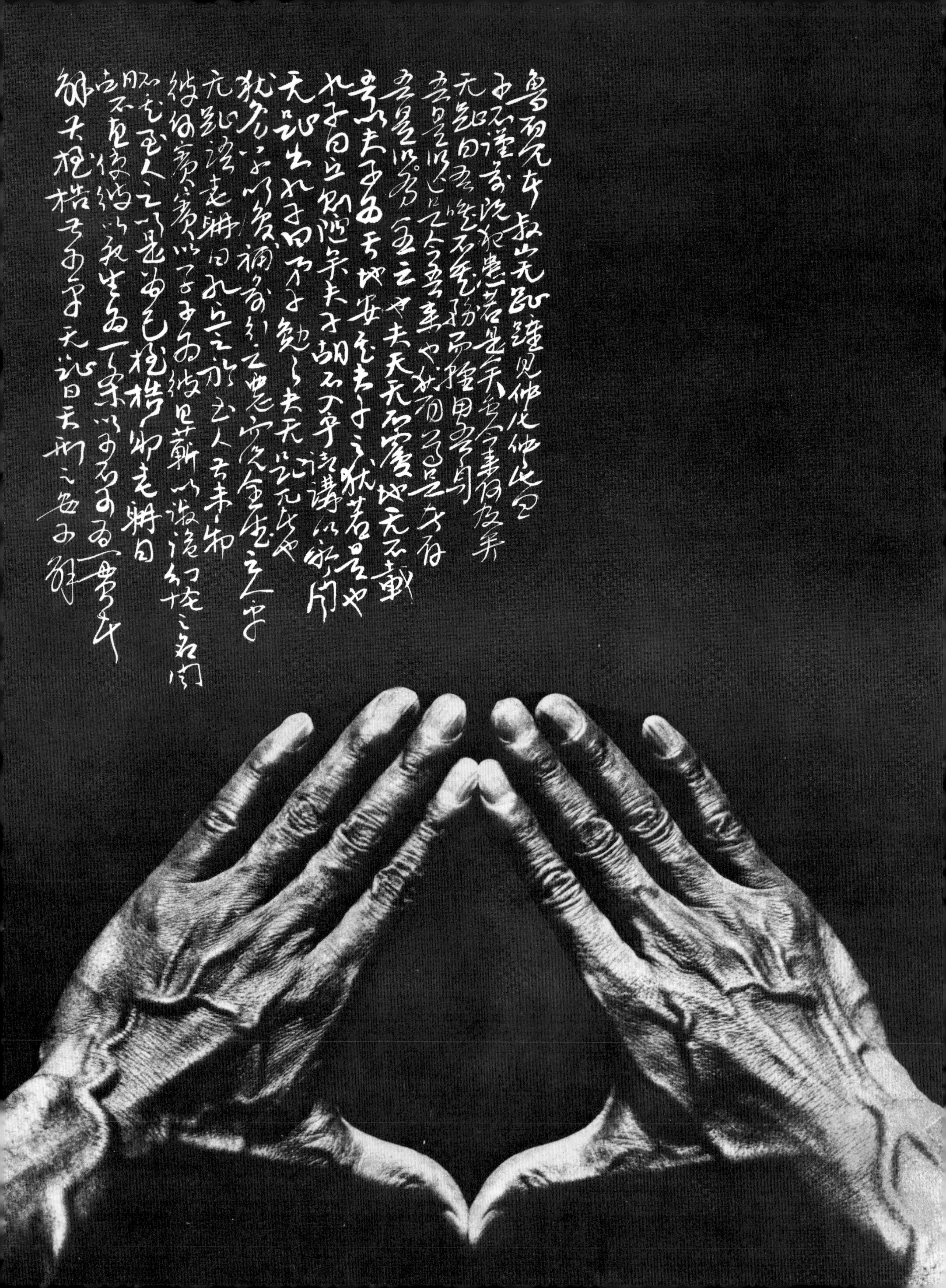

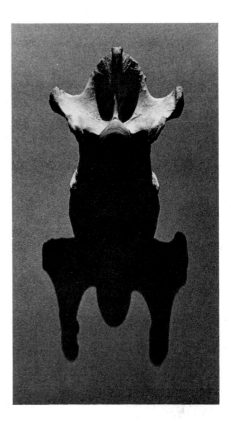

There was a cripple in Lu named Shu Shan No-toes. He came walking on his heels to see Confucius. Confucius said, "You did not take care. You committed a crime and brought this trouble upon yourself. What is the use of coming to me now?"

No-toes said, "I didn't know how to behave properly, and took my body lightly, so I lost my toes. I have come here with something more precious than toes, and it is this which I seek to preserve. There is nothing that heaven does not cover. There is nothing that earth does not sustain. I thought that you, Master, were like heaven and earth. How was I to know that you would receive me this way?"

Confucius said, "It was stupid of me. Why don't you come in! Let us talk."

But No-toes walked out.

Confucius said, "This is a good lesson, disciples! A toeless cripple is still willing to atone for his past misdeeds. How much more can be done by those who haven't had such bad luck."

No-toes went to see Lao Tsu and said, "Is Confucius not yet a perfect man? Why does he keep imitating you? He is trying to gain a reputation by pretending to know strange and extraordinary things. He does not know that real sages look upon these as cuffs and fetters."

Lao Tsu said, "Why don't you simply make him see that life and death are one thread, the same line viewed from different sides—and thus free him from his cuffs and fetters? Is that possible?"

No-toes said, "If heaven wants to punish him, who can free him?"

Duke Ai of Lu asked Confucius, "In Wei, there was an ugly man by the name of Ai Tai To. Yet the men around him thought so much of him, they could never leave him. When young ladies saw him, they told their parents that they would rather be his concubines than other men's wives. There were ten or more such cases. He never tried to lead others but always went along with people. He was never in the position of a ruler who could protect people's lives. He was not a wealthy man who could fill people's bellies. Moreover, he was hideous enough to scare everything under heaven. He agreed with people but never persuaded them. He knew only what happened in the place where he lived. Yet both men and women sought his company. There must have been something extraordinary about him, I thought. So I summoned him for an interview, and indeed he was frighteningly ugly. Yet within the first month that he was with me, I began to see that there was something in that man, and within a year I completely trusted him. As my state needed a Prime Minister, I offered him the position. He was reluctant to give a reply, and was evasive as though he wanted to refuse. That made me feel ashamed, and finally I handed over the government to him. Soon after that, he went away and left me. I was so sad, it was as if I were in mourning. I no longer had anyone with whom I could share the joy of my state. What kind of man was that?"

Confucius said, "Once when I was on a mission to the state of Chu, I saw some little pigs sucking their dead mother. After a while, they suddenly looked at her. Then they all ran away and left her because she did not look back at them. She was no longer like themselves. What they loved in their mother was not her body but that which made her body alive. When a man is killed in battle and is buried, he has no use for medals. When a man has no feet, he does not care about shoes. Both men have lost something essential. The King's concubines do not trim their nails or pierce their ears. When a man is newly married, he stays away from his official duties and is not sent on missions. Such is the importance of keeping the body whole. How much more important to preserve virtue. Now, Ai Tai To said nothing and was trusted. He achieved nothing and was loved. So someone offered him the government, and was only afraid that he would refuse. He must have achieved full harmony without any outward manifestation of virtue."

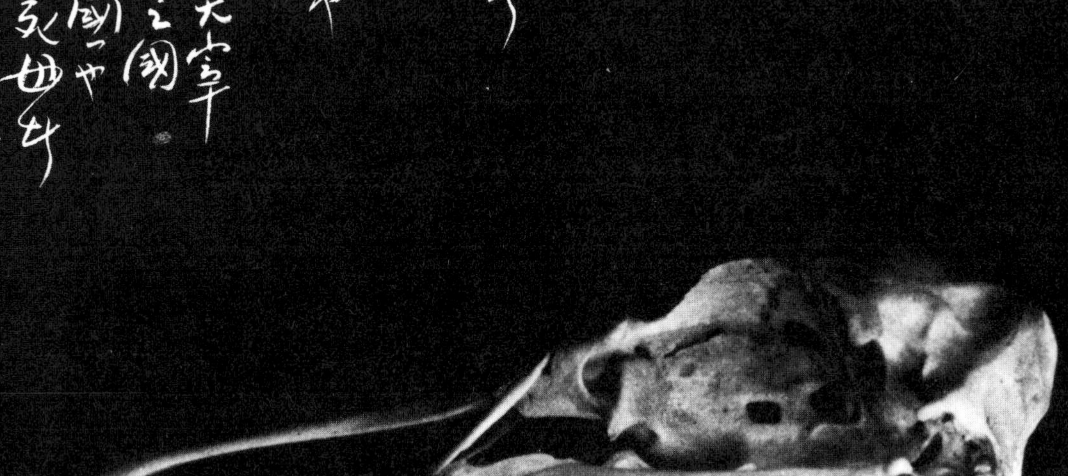

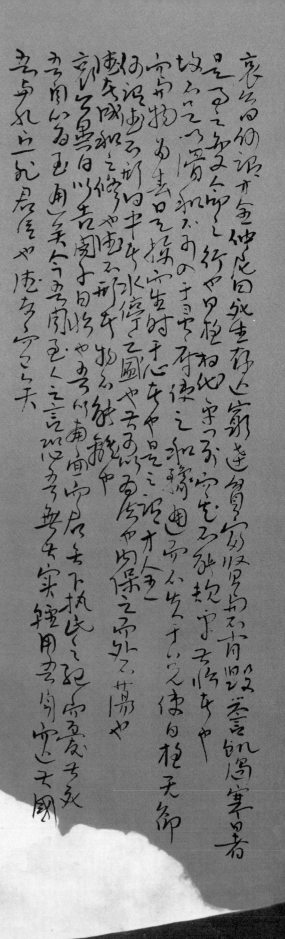

莊子之楚，見空髑髏，髐然有形，撽以馬捶，因而問之，曰：「夫子貪生失理，而為此乎？將子有亡國之事，斧鉞之誅，而為此乎？將子有不善之行，愧遺父母妻子之醜，而為此乎？將子有凍餒之患，而為此乎？將子之春秋故及此乎？」於是語卒，援髑髏，枕而臥。

夜半，髑髏見夢曰：「子之談者似辯士。視子所言，皆生人之累也，死則無此矣。子欲聞死之說乎？」莊子曰：「然。」髑髏曰：「死，無君於上，無臣於下；亦無四時之事，從然以天地為春秋，雖南面王樂，不能過也。」

莊子不信，曰：「吾使司命復生子形，為子骨肉肌膚，反子父母妻子閭里知識，子欲之乎？」髑髏深矉蹙頞曰：「吾安能棄南面王樂，而復為人間之勞乎！」

Duke Ai asked, "What do you mean by achieving full harmony?"

Confucius said, "Life and death, profit and loss, failure and success, poverty and wealth, value and worthlessness, praise and blame, hunger and thirst, cold and heat—these are natural changes in the order of things. They alternate with one another like day and night. No one knows where one ends and the other begins. Therefore, they should not disturb our peace or enter into our souls. Live so that you are at ease, in harmony with the world, and full of joy. Day and night, share the springtime with all things, thus creating the seasons in your own heart. This is called achieving full harmony."

"And what is this lack of outward manifestation of virtue?"

Confucius said, "Balance is the perfect state of still water. Let that be our model. It remains quiet within and is not disturbed on the surface. Virtue is the attainment of perfect harmony. Because virtue has no outward form, nothing can escape from it."

Later, Duke Ai told this to Ming Tsu, saying, "When I first faced south and took the reins of government, guiding the people and caring for their lives, I thought that I was doing my utmost as a ruler. Now that I have heard the words of a perfect man, I am afraid that there is no substance to what I am doing. I have foolishly squandered my energy and am ruining my country. Confucius and I are no longer related as subject and ruler but as spiritual companions."

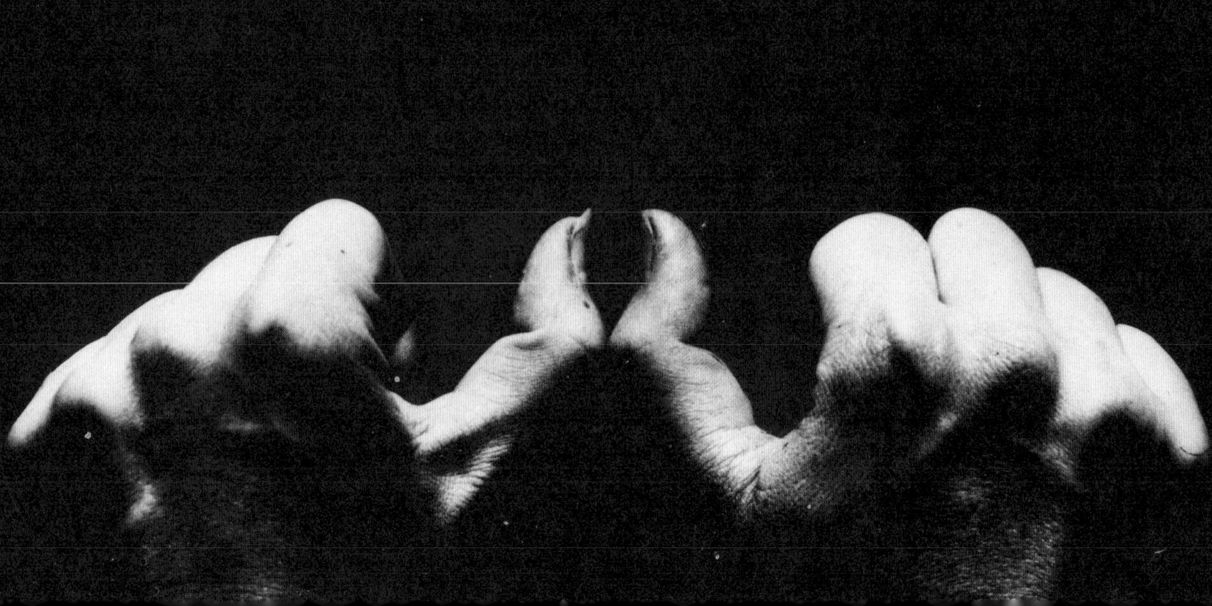

Clubfoot-Hunchback-No-lips talked to Duke Ling of Wei. Duke Ling was so delighted with him that when he saw normal people, their necks appeared thin and scraggy. Jug-Jar-Big-goiter talked to Duke Huan of Chi. Duke Huan was so delighted with him that when he saw normal people, he too thought their necks were thin and scraggy. So when goodness shines forth, the outward appearances are forgotten. Men do not forget what ought to be forgotten, but forget what ought not be forgotten. This is forgetfulness indeed! Therefore, the sage lets everything pass before his mind. To him learning is something added, conventions are like glue, morality is a bond, and skills are for trade. The sage does not make plans, so what use has he for learning? He does not make divisions, so what use has he for glue? He lacks nothing, so what use has he for morality? He has nothing to sell, so what use has he for trade? His not needing these four things is a gift from heaven. This gift is his heavenly food. Since he is fed by heaven, what use has he for men? He has the appearance of a man but not the desires of a man. He has the appearance of a man, so he associates with men. He does not have the desires of a man, so he is not concerned with right or wrong. How infinitely small is that which makes him a man! How infinitely great is that which makes him perfect in heaven!

Hui Tsu asked Chuang Tsu, "Can a man really live without desire?"

"Yes," said Chuang Tsu.

"But," said Hui Tsu, "if a man has no desire, how can you call him a man?"

Chuang Tsu said, "Tao gives him his appearance, and heaven gives him his body. Why should he not be called a man?"

Hui Tsu said, "Since he is called a man, how can he be without desire?"

Chuang Tsu said, "That is not what I mean by desire. When I say he has no desire I mean that he does not disturb his inner well-being with likes and dislikes. He accepts things as they are and does not try to improve upon them."

Hui Tsu said, "If a man does not try to improve upon the way things are, how does he survive?"

Chuang Tsu said, "Tao gives him his appearance. Heaven gives him his body. He does not disturb his inner well-being with likes and dislikes. At present you use all your vital energy on external things and wear out your spirit. You lean against a tree and mutter, collapse upon a rotten stump and fall asleep. Your body is a gift from heaven, yet you use it to babble and jabber about 'hardness' and 'whiteness'!"

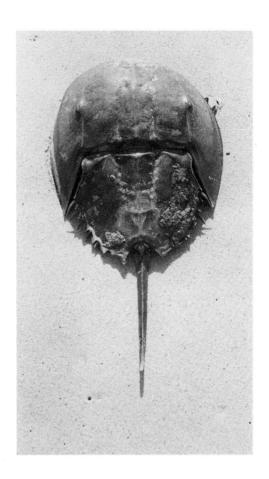

患者謂莊子曰人皆有七情何以謂之人
莊子曰然患者莫非七情之所患者何以謂之患者
莊者曰然患者莫非情乎患者謂之七情乎
患者身莫能定之乎
患者身莫能定之乎
莊者身道句之觀天莫之非天以好患者肉傷乎身
今子知患子之即莫事子之精停撗
天此豈足之所也則出照知也

停撗
宿嶐擦撗而臚

CHAPTER SIX

THE GREAT MASTER

知天之所為、知人之所為者、至矣。知天之所為者、天而生也。知人之所為者、以其知之所知、以養其知之所不知、終其天年而不中道夭者、是知之盛也。雖然、有患。夫知有所待而後當、其所待者特未定也。庸詎知吾所謂天之非人乎、所謂人之非天乎。

Perfect is the man who knows what comes
from heaven and what comes from man.
Knowing what comes from heaven, he is
in tune with heaven. Knowing what
comes from man, he uses his knowledge
of the known to develop his knowledge
of the unknown and enjoys the fullness of
life until his natural death. This is the
perfection of knowledge. However, there
is one difficulty. Knowledge must be
based upon something, but one is not
certain what this may be. How, indeed,
do I know that what I call heaven is not
actually man, and that what I call man is
not actually heaven? First, there must be
a true man; then there can be true
knowledge.

But what is a true man? The true man of old did not mind being poor. He took no pride in his achievements. He made no plans. Thus, he could commit an error and not regret it. He could succeed without being proud. Thus, he could climb mountains without fear, enter water without getting wet, and pass through fire unscathed. This is the knowledge that leads to Tao.

The true man of old slept without dreaming and woke without anxiety. His food was plain, and his breath was deep. For the breath of the true man rose up from his heels while the breath of common men rises from their throats. When they are overcome, their words catch in their throats like vomit. As their lusts and desires deepen, their heavenly nature grows shallow.

The true man of old knew nothing about loving life or hating death. When he was born, he felt no elation. When he entered death, there was no sorrow. Carefree he went. Carefree he came. That was all. He did not forget his beginning and did not seek his end. He accepted what he was given with delight, and when it was gone, he gave it no more thought. This is called not using the mind against Tao and not using man to help heaven. Such was the true man.

何謂真人古之真人不逆寡不雄成不謨士若然
者過而弗悔當而不自得也若然者登高不慄
入水不濡入火不熱是知之能登假於道者也若此
古之真人其寢不夢其覺無憂其食不甘其息深深
真人之息以踵眾人之息以喉屈服者其嗌言若哇
其耆欲深者其天機淺古之真人不知說生不知惡
死其出不訢其入不距翛然而往翛然而來而已矣
不忘其所始不求其所終受而喜之忘而復之是之謂
不以心捐道不以人助天是之謂真人

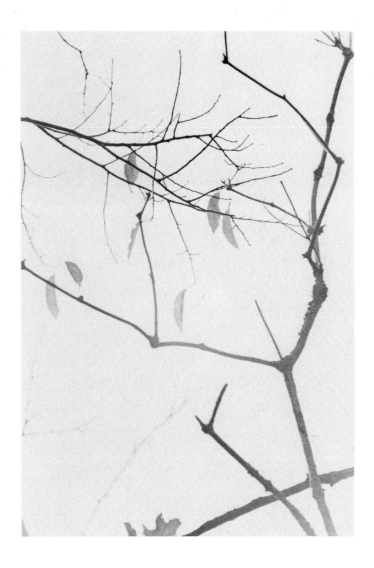

Such a man has a free mind, a calm manner, and an unfurrowed brow. He is as cool as autumn and as mild as spring. His joy and anger flow like changing seasons. He is in harmony with all things and has no limitations. Therefore, when a wise man wages war, he can destroy a nation without losing the people's hearts. His blessings fall upon the ten thousand things, but not because he loves men.

Therefore, the man who desires to know all things is not a sage. Showing partiality is not true kindness. He who calculates his timing is not a man of wisdom. He who does not see through gain and loss is not a great man. He who seeks recognition and does not follow what he knows is not a man of understanding. He who would lose his life without being true to himself can never be a master of men. Such men as Hu Pu Chieh, Wu Kuang, Po I, Shu Chi, Chi Tsu, Hsu Yu, Chi To, and Shen Tu Ti all lost their lives by doing the bidding of others. They tried to act in ways that were natural to others but not natural to themselves.

This was the true man of old. He stood straight and firm and did not waver. He was of humble mien but was not servile. He was independent but not stubborn, open to everything yet made no boast. He smiled as if pleased, and responded to things naturally. His radiance came from his inner light. He remained centered even in the company of others. He was broadminded as if he agreed with everyone, high-minded as if beyond influence, inward-minded as if he would like to withdraw from the world, and absent-minded as if unaware of what he was going to say. He considered criminal law to be the body of government, ceremony its wings, knowledge a requirement of the times, and reason a guide for action. To consider law as the body, one has to be lenient in its execution. To take ceremony as the wings is to give people something to follow. To take knowledge as a requirement of the times is to do things that have to be done. To consider reason as a guide for action is to be with others on the path upward. He acted effortlessly, yet people thought that he was trying very hard.

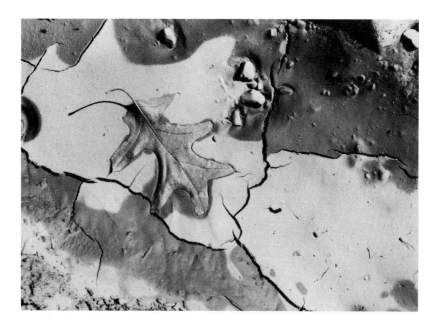

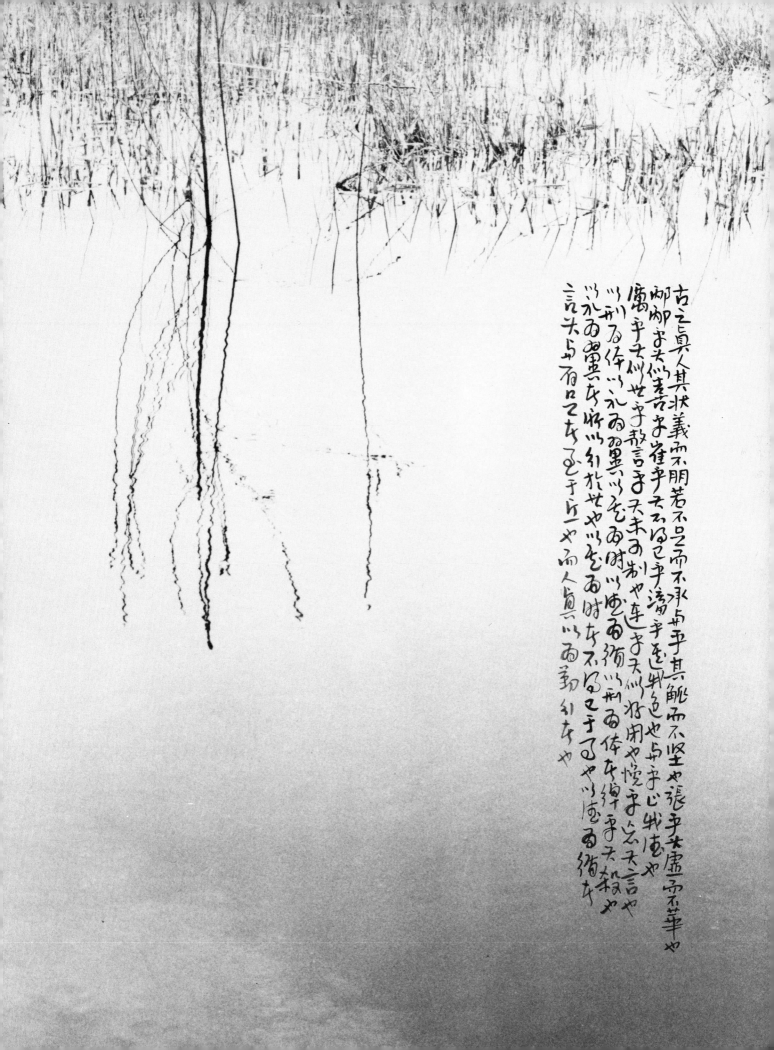

What he likes is the One; what he does not like is also the One. That which is One is One; that which is not One is also One. He knows the One and is of heaven. He knows not the One and is of men. So heaven and men are not in conflict. Such is the true man. It is destiny to live and die, as certain as night and day. It is of heaven, beyond the interference of men.

Such is the nature of things. If a man is willing to view heaven as his father and experiences love, how much more love will he feel for what is beyond heaven! If he feels that the ruler of the kingdom is above him and he is willing to die for the king, how much more will he be willing to do for the truth!

When the springs go dry and fish are left stranded on the ground, they smear each other with slime and spew spit on one another. It is better for them to be in the rivers and lakes, where they pay each other no heed. Instead of praising Yao and denouncing Chieh, it would be better to pay heed to neither and lose one-self in Tao.

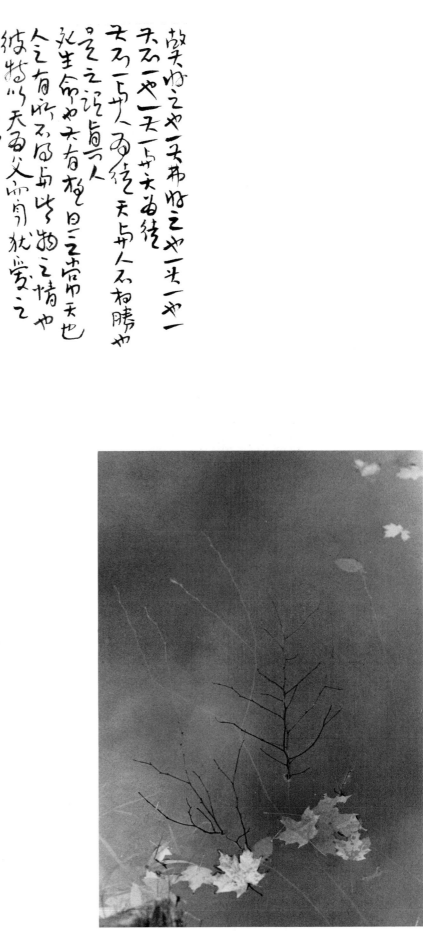

故矣かこ也や天亦ぬこや天こや天こや
天こや天こや天亦由徒
天こ与人有徒天与人不相勝や
是之謂旨人
死生命也天有権日こ常也天也
人之有所不届あひ物之情や
彼物以天西父而旬犹爱之
向况天卓や
人特以有子西愈こ而况天真こ乎
泉涸魚相与処于陸相喣以湿相濡以沫不
如相忘于江湖与其誉尭而非桀
不如两忘而化其道

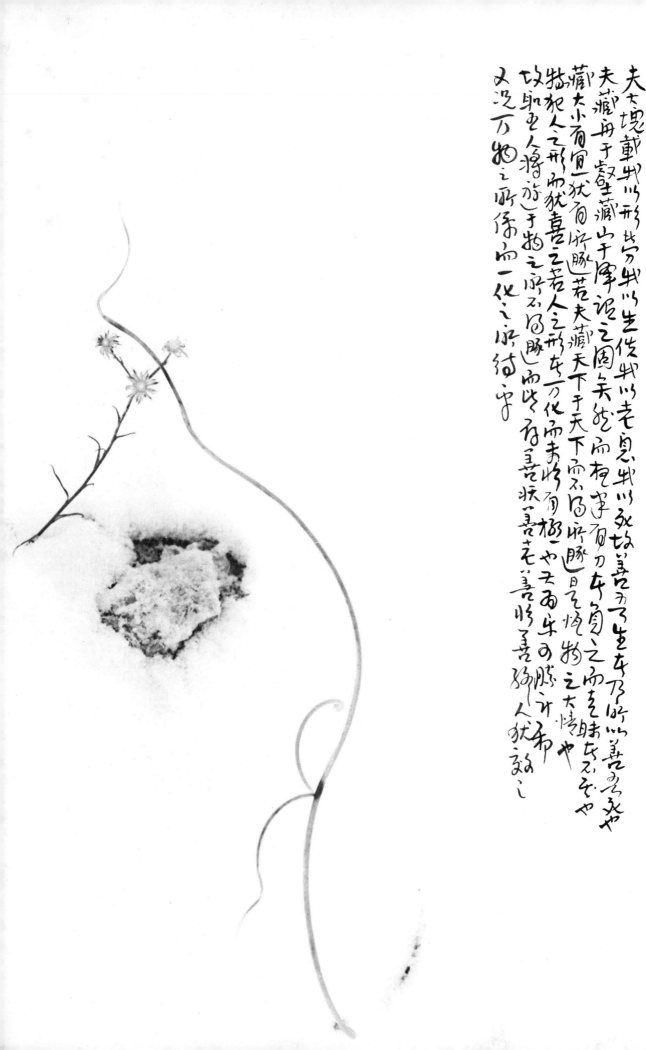

夫大塊載我以形　勞我以生　佚我以老　息我以死　故善吾生者　乃所以善吾死也
夫藏舟於壑　藏山於澤　謂之固矣　然而夜半有力者負之而走　昧者不知也
藏小大有宜　猶有所遯　若夫藏天下於天下而不得所遯　是恆物之大情也
特犯人之形而猶喜之　若人之形者　萬化而未始有極也　其為樂可勝計邪
故聖人將遊於物之所不得遯而皆存　善妖善老　善始善終　人猶效之
又況萬物之所係　而一化之所待乎

The great earth burdens me with a body, causes me to toil in life, eases me in old age, and rests me in death. That which makes my life good, makes my death good also.

A boat concealed in a ravine and a fish net in a swamp appear to be safely hidden. But at midnight a strong man may put them on his back and walk off with them. Dimwits do not understand that no matter how well one hides small things in larger ones, there is always a chance of losing them. But if you hide the universe in the universe, there is no way to lose it. This is the ultimate reality.

You were born in a human form, and you find joy in it. Yet there are ten thousand other forms endlessly transforming that are equally good, and the joy in these is untold. The sage dwells among those things which can never be lost, and so he lives forever. He willingly accepts early death, old age, the beginning and the end, and serves as an example for everyone. How much more should we emulate the creator of the ten thousand things, on whom the great flow depends!

Tao has reality and substance, but no action or form. It can be given but not received. It is attainable but invisible. It is its own source and its own root. It existed before heaven and earth and for all eternity. It causes spirits and gods to be divine. It begets heaven and earth. It is above the zenith and yet not high. It is below the nadir and yet not low. It was born before heaven and earth but not long ago. It was there before the oldest antiquity but is not old.

Hsi Wei attained Tao and brought heaven and earth into harmony. Fu Hsi attained it and entered into the source of vital energy. The Great Bear attained it and has never erred from its course. The sun and moon attained it and have never ceased to shine. Kan Pi attained it and entered Kunlun Mountain. Feng I attained it and wandered along the Great River. Chien Wu attained it and dwelt on Mount Tai. The Yellow Emperor attained it and soared upon the clouds to heaven. Chuan Hsu attained it and dwelt in the Dark Palace. Yu Chiang attained it and went to live at the North Pole. The Queen Mother of the West attained it and took her seat on Shao Kwan Mountain. No one knows her beginning and no one knows her end. Peng Tsu attained it and lived from the time of Shun to the time of the Five Princes. Fu Yueh attained it, became Prime Minister to Wu Ting, and ruled the world. Then he mounted the eastern Milky Way, and riding on Sagittarius and Scorpio, he took his place among the constellations.

Nan Po Tsu Kuei asked Hunchback Woman, "You are old, and yet you look like a child. Why is this?"

"I have found Tao," she replied.

"Can Tao be learned?" he asked.

"No! How could it be? You are not the one to do it, anyway. Now, consider Pu Liang I. He has the talent of a sage but not the Tao of a sage. I have the Tao of a sage but not the talent. I wished to teach him so that he might indeed be a sage. Teaching the Tao of a sage to one who has the talent of a sage seems to be an easy matter. But no, it took a long time to reveal it to him. After three days, he began to transcend the physical world. After his transcendence of the physical world, I kept working with him. After seven days, he began to transcend all material existence. After his transcendence of all material existence, I kept working with him. After nine days, he began to transcend all life. Having transcended all life, he began to achieve the clear vision of dawn. Having achieved the clear vision of dawn, he began to see the One. Having seen the One, he began to transcend the distinction of past and present. Having transcended the distinction of past and present, he began to enter the land where there is no life or death, where killing does not take away life and giving birth does not add to it. He would reject nothing, welcomed all things, negated all things, and affirmed all things. This is called tranquillity in struggle, meaning perfection is the result of struggle."

Nan Po Tsu Kuei asked, "Where did you learn all this?"

She replied, "I have learned it from the son of Ink-writing, the son of Ink-writing from the grandson of Chanting-recitation, the grandson of Chanting-recitation from Clear-understanding, Clear-understanding from Quiet-affirmation, Quiet-affirmation from Immediate-experience, Immediate-experience from Dramatic-expression, Dramatic-expression from Dark-obscurity, Dark-obscurity from Mysterious-void, and Mysterious-void from Beginning-of-no-beginning."

Four men, Tsu Szu, Tsu Yu, Tsu Li, and Tsu Lai, were having a discussion, saying, "Whoever believes Nothingness to be the head, Life to be the backbone, and Death to be the tail; whoever can know life, death, being, and non-being all as one, shall be our friend." The four looked at one another and smiled. And since they were in complete agreement, they became fast friends.

Not long after, Tsu Yu fell ill, and Tsu Szu went to see him. Tsu Yu said, "Great is the Maker of Things that He should make me as deformed as this!"

His crooked spine was curled round like a hunchback; his five organs were upside down; his chin rested on his navel; his shoulders rose up above his head; his neckbone pointed to the sky. His body was sick, yet he was calm and carefree. He limped to the well and looked at his reflection and said, "Ah! The Maker of Things has made me all crooked like this!"

"Does this upset you?" asked Tsu Szu.

"No, why should it? If my left arm became a rooster, I would use it to herald the dawn. If my right arm became a crossbow, I would shoot down a bird for roasting. If my buttocks became wheels and my spirits a horse, I would ride them. What need would I have for a wagon? For we were born because it was time, and we die in accordance with nature. If we are content with whatever happens and follow the flow, joy and sorrow cannot affect us. This is what the ancients called freedom from bondage. There are those who cannot free themselves because they are bound by material existence. But nothing can overcome heaven. That is the way it has always been. Why should I be upset?"

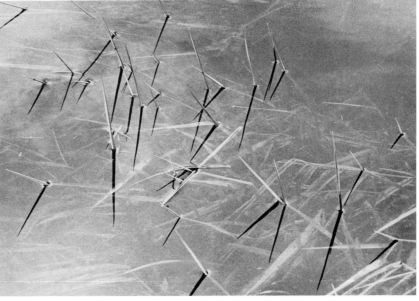

莊子妻死，惠子弔之，莊子則方箕踞鼓盆而歌。惠子曰：「與人居，長子、老、身死，不哭亦足矣，又鼓盆而歌，不亦甚乎！」

莊子曰：「不然。是其始死也，我獨何能無概然！察其始而本無生，非徒無生也而本無形，非徒無形也而本無氣。雜乎芒芴之間，變而有氣，氣變而有形，形變而有生，今又變而之死，是相與為春秋冬夏四時行也。人且偃然寢於巨室，而我噭噭然隨而哭之，自以為不通乎命，故止也。」

Shortly, thereafter, Tsu Lai fell ill. He lay gasping for life while his wife and children gathered around crying. Tsu Li came to see him and said, "Shhh! Get away from him! Do not disturb the transformation!" Leaning against the door, he said to Tsu Lai, "Great is the Maker! What will He use you for now? Where will He send you? Will He make you into a rat's gizzard or a snake's leg?"

Tsu Lai replied, "A son must go wherever his parents tell him to go! East, west, south, or north. Yin and Yang are no other than one's parents. If they brought me to the verge of death and I do not obey them, then I am only being stubborn. They are not to be blamed.

The great earth burdens me with a body, causes me to toil in life, eases me in old age, and rests me in death. That which makes my life good makes my death good also. If a skilled smith were casting metal and the metal should leap up and say, 'Make me into a famous sword like Mo Yeh!' the smith would surely consider it an ill omen. Now, if by chance I were being cast into a human form and I were to say, 'Make me a man! Make me a man!' the Maker of Things would certainly consider me an ill omen. Now, if I regard heaven and earth as a great melting pot and creation and transformation as a master smith, then where can I be sent and not find it fitting? Thus, calmly I sleep and freshly I waken."

子桑戶子孟子反子琴張三人相與友
曰孰能相與於無相與相為於無相為
孰能登天遊霧撓挑無極
相忘以生無所終窮
三人相視而笑莫逆於心
遂相與為友莫然有間
而子桑戶死未葬
孔子聞之使子貢往侍事焉
或編曲或鼓琴
相和而歌曰嗟來桑戶乎嗟來桑戶乎而已反其真
而我猶為人猗子貢趨而進曰敢問臨尸而歌禮乎
二人相視而笑曰是惡知禮意

Tsu Sang Hu, Meng Tsu Fan, and Tsu Chin Chang were acquaintances. They said to each other, "Who can be together without togetherness and cooperate without cooperation? Who can soar up to heaven, wander through the clouds, and pass beyond the limits of space, unmindful of existence, forever and ever?" Then the three looked at one another and laughed. Having no disagreement among themselves, they became fast friends.

After some time, Tsu Sang Hu died. Before the burial, Confucius heard of his death and sent his disciple Tsu Kung to attend the mourning. Tsu Kung found that one of the friends was composing a song and the other was playing a lute.

They sang together in unison, "Oh Sang Hu! Oh Sang Hu! You have gone back to your true self while we remain as men. Alas! Alas!"

Tsu Kung hurried in and said, "May I ask something? Is that appropriate, singing in the presence of a corpse?"

The two looked at each other and laughed. "What does he know about ceremony?" they said.

子貢反以告孔子曰、彼何人者邪、修行无有、而外其形骸、臨尸而歌、顏色不變、无以命之、彼何人者邪、孔子曰、彼遊方之外者也、而丘遊方之內者也、外內不相及、而丘使女往弔之、丘則陋矣、彼方且與造物者為人、而遊乎天地之一氣、彼以生為附贅縣疣、以死為決𤷾潰癰、夫若然者、又惡知死生先後之所在、假於異物、託於同體、忘其肝膽、遺其耳目、反覆終始、不知端倪、芒然彷徨乎塵垢之外、逍遙乎无為之業、彼又惡能憒憒然為世俗之禮、以觀眾人之耳目哉、子貢曰、然則夫子何方之依、孔子曰、丘、天之戮民也、雖然、吾與汝共之、子貢曰、敢問其方、孔子曰、魚相造乎水、人相造乎道、相造乎水者、穿池而養給、相造乎道者、无事而生定、故曰、魚相忘乎江湖、人相忘乎道術、子貢曰、敢問畸人、曰、畸人者、畸於人而侔於天、故曰、天之小人、人之君子、天之君子、人之小人也

Tsu Kung went back and reported to Confucius, saying, "What sort of men are they? They are badly behaved and are unconcerned with appearances. They sang in front of the corpse with no sign of emotion. I do not know how to describe them. What sort of people are they?"

Confucius said, "They travel beyond the physical world, and I travel within it. Our paths will never meet. It was stupid of me to send you to attend the funeral. They are now in the company of the Maker of Things and are taking delight in the one breath of heaven and earth. They look upon life as a swelling tumor, a protruding goiter, and look upon death as the bursting of a boil and the draining of an abscess. How could such men discriminate between life and death? They consider the body as an accidental arrangement of different elements. They forget their livers and galls, and ignore their eyes and ears. They come and go, ending and beginning again, unmindful of any limitations. Without a care, they roam beyond the dusty world and wander freely, dwelling in non-action. Why should they bother with the conventions of this vulgar world and make a show for the eyes and ears of the common people?"

Tsu Kung said, "Why then, Master, do you observe conventions?"

Confucius said, "I am condemned by heaven to do so. However, you and I have this in common."

Tsu Kung said, "May I ask what you mean?"

Confucius said, "Fish thrive in water; men thrive in Tao. Those who thrive in water dart about in the pond and find nourishment there. Those who

thrive in Tao work without doing, and their nature is realized. Therefore, it is said, 'Fish need to lose themselves in rivers and lakes, and men need to lose themselves in the practice of Tao.' "

Tsu Kung said, "May I ask about those strange people?"

"The strange people are strange to men but familiar to heaven. Therefore, it is said, 'The inferior man of heaven is superior among men; the inferior man among men is superior in heaven.' "

Yen Hui asked Confucius, "When Meng Sun Tsai's mother died, he cried out but did not weep. He was not sad at heart. He observed mourning without sorrow. With these three failings, he was nevertheless considered the best mourner in the state of Lu. How can one gain such a reputation on nothing? I am utterly amazed!"

Confucius said, "Meng Sun has indeed mastered Tao! He has gone beyond wisdom. He has already made his life simple. Yet there are certain customs he still has to observe. Meng Sun does not know why we live and why we die. He does not know which comes first and which last. He accepts his state of being without concern for future transformation. When one is changing, how does one know that a change is taking place? When one is not changing, how does one know that a change hasn't already occurred? Maybe you and I are still in a dream and have not yet awakened. Moreover, Meng Sun appeared shaken, but his mind was not moved. There was a change of abode, but there was no real death. Meng Sun was the only one who was awake. He wept only when he saw the others weep; that is his true nature. Furthermore, we all talk about 'me.' How do we know that there is such a person as 'me'? You dream that you are a bird soaring up to the sky. You dream that you are a fish diving in a pool. As we speak now, we do not know whether we are awake or dreaming. Making accusations is not as good as laughing. And laughter is not as good as letting things follow their natural course. Be content with what is happening and forget about change; then you can enter into the oneness of the mystery of heaven."

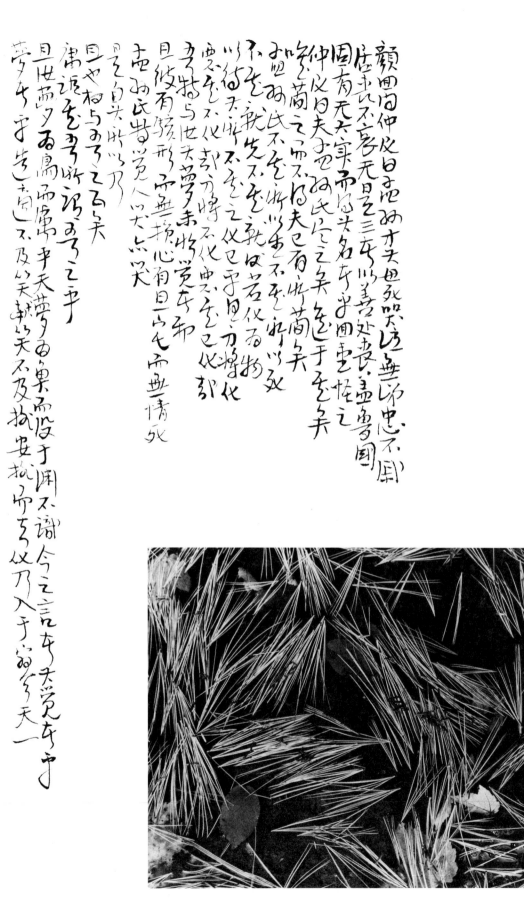

Yi Erh Tsu went to see Hsu Yu. Hsu Yu asked, "What has Yao taught you?"

Yi Erh Tsu said, "Yao instructed me to practice kindness and goodness and to distinguish clearly between right and wrong."

Hsu Yu said, "Then why do you come to see me? Yao has already branded you with kindness and goodness and cut off your nose with right and wrong. How will you be able to wander on the path, freely and without a care, doing whatever you like?"

Yi Erh Tsu said, "That may be so, but I would still like to wander along the fringes if I can."

Hsu Yu said, "No, when a man is blind, it is impossible for him to appreciate the beauty of face and complexion or to tell a blue sacrificial robe from a yellow one."

Yi Erh Tsu said, "Wu Chuang surrendered her beauty, Chu Liang abandoned his strength, and the Yellow Emperor discarded his knowledge. All of these were part of a process of purging and purification. How do you know that the Maker of Things would not rid me of my brands, replace my nose, and make me fit to be your disciple?"

Hsu Yu said, "Ah! We cannot tell yet. But let me give you the general idea. O my master! O my master! he set the ten thousand things in order, yet he does not consider himself good. He gave life to the ten thousand generations, yet he does not consider himself kind. He is more ancient than the oldest antiquity, yet he does not consider himself old. He covers heaven, sustains the earth, carves and fashions all forms, yet he does not consider himself skillful. I follow him."

堯讓天下於許由曰日月出矣而爝火不息其於光也不亦難乎時雨降矣而猶浸灌其於澤也不亦勞乎夫子立而天下治而我猶尸之吾自視缺然請致天下許由曰子治天下天下既已治也而我猶代子吾將為名乎名者實之賓也吾將為賓乎鷦鷯巢於深林不過一枝偃鼠飲河不過滿腹歸休乎君予無所用天下為庖人雖不治庖尸祝不越樽俎而代之矣

Yen Hui said, "I am making progress."

Confucius asked, "In what way?"

Yen Hui said, "I have given up doing good and being right."

Confucius said, "Very good, but that is not quite enough."

Another day, Yen Hui saw Confucius and said, "I am making progress."

Confucius asked, "In what way?"

Yen Hui said, "I have given up ceremony and music."

Confucius said, "Very good, but that is not quite enough."

Another day, Yen Hui saw Confucius again and said, "I am making progress."

Confucius asked, "In what way?"

Yen Hui said, "I just sit and forget."

Confucius was startled and asked, "What do you mean by sitting and forgetting?"

Yen Hui said, "I am not attached to the body and I give up any idea of knowing. By freeing myself from the body and mind, I become one with the infinite. This is what I mean by sitting and forgetting."

Confucius said, "When there is oneness, there are no preferences. When there is change, there is no constancy. If you have really attained this, then let me become your pupil."

Tsu Yu and Tsu Sang were friends. Once when it had rained for ten days, Tsu Yu said, "Tsu Sang may be having a hard time." So he packed up some food and took it to him. Arriving at Tsu Sang's door, he heard something that was like singing or weeping, accompanied by a lute. "O Father! O Mother! Is it heaven? Or is it man?" The voice was breaking, and the words faltered.

Tsu Yu entered and said, "Why are you chanting poetry like this?"

Tsu Sang said, "I am trying to find out why I am in such a wretched state. I cannot understand it. Would my father and mother have wanted me to be so poor? Heaven provides shelter for things. Earth sustains all things. Would heaven and earth single me out to be poor? I am trying to find the cause of this but cannot see what it is. Yet here I am in my wretchedness. It must be fate."

庵帝王

CHAPTER SEVEN

THE SAGE KING

Yeh Chueh was questioning Wang Yi. Four times he asked a question and four times he received no answer. This delighted Yeh Chueh so much, he went to tell Pu Yi Tsu.

Pu Yi Tsu said, "Are you only just finding that out? Emperor Shun was no match for Emperor Fu Shi. Emperor Shun always tried to do good so that men would follow him. He was never able to distinguish between what a man is and what he is not. On the other hand, Emperor Fu Shi was calm and tranquil when asleep, and simple and direct when awake. Sometimes he would take on the spirit of a horse, and sometimes that of an ox. His wisdom could be trusted. His virtue was genuine. He was beyond distinguishing between what a man is and what he is not."

肩吾見狂接輿狂接輿曰日中始何以語女
肩吾曰告我君人者以己出經式義度
人孰敢不聽而化諸
狂接輿曰是欺德也
其於治天下也猶涉海鑿河而使蚉負山也
夫聖人之治也治外乎
正而後行
確乎能其事者而已矣
且鳥高飛以避矰弋之害
鼷鼠深穴乎神丘之下
以避熏鑿之患
而曾二蟲之無知

Chien Wu went to see the madman, Chieh Yu. Chieh Yu said, "What did Chung Shih tell you the other day?"

Chien Wu said, "He told me that a ruler should be an example to others, establishing law and order, ceremony, and measure, so that every man is influenced and is never tempted to break the law."

Chieh Yu said, "This is subverting virtue! Trying to govern the world that way is like wading through the sea, digging a river, or making a mosquito carry a mountain on its back. When a wise man rules, is he concerned with outward appearances? When the mind is clear, then appropriate action follows. Let each man do what he can, that is all. Birds fly high in the sky so as to avoid being hit by stringed arrows. Mice make their homes deep under the sacred mound so as to avoid being smoked out or dug up. Surely men have more sense than these two creatures?"

Tien Ken was traveling on the south side of Mount Yin. When he reached the Liao River, he met a nameless sage to whom he said, "Please tell me how to rule the world."

The nameless sage said, "Go away, you fool! Why do you ask such an improper question? I am about to join the Maker of Things. For enjoyment I ride on the bird of ease and emptiness, out beyond the six directions, wandering in the land of nowhere and dwelling in the domain of nothingness. Why do you bother me with the problem of ruling the world?"

But Tien Ken repeated his question once more. The nameless sage said, "Let your mind wander in the pure and simple. Be one with the infinite. Allow all things to take their course. Do not try to be clever. Then the world will be ruled!"

天根遊於殷陽，至蓼水之上，適遭無名人而問焉，曰：「請問為天下。」無名人曰：「去！汝鄙人也，何問之不豫也！予方將與造物者為人，厭則又乘夫莽眇之鳥，以出六極之外，而遊無何有之鄉，以處壙埌之野。汝又何帠以治天下感予之心為？」又復問。無名人曰：「汝遊心於淡，合氣於漠，順物自然而無容私焉，而天下治矣。」

Yang Tsu Chu went to see Lao Tsu and said, "Here is a man who is sensitive, alert, strong, and decisive, with a thorough knowledge of the workings of things and untiring in his study of Tao. Could he be compared with a sage king?"

Lao Tsu said, "In comparison with the sages, such a man is like a hard-working servant, a craftsman intent upon his work, wearing out his body and confusing his mind. It is said that the reason men hunt the tiger and the leopard is the beauty of their skins. The agility of the monkey and the dog's ability to catch rats cause men to domesticate them. So how can such a man be compared with a sage king?"

Yang Tsu Chu was amazed and said, "May I ask how a sage king rules?"

Lao Tsu said, "When a sage king rules, his influence is felt everywhere but he does not seem to be doing anything. His work affects the ten thousand things, but the people do not depend upon him. No one is aware of him, but he brings happiness to every man. He stands on that which is not known and wanders in the land of nowhere."

In the state of Cheng, there was a shaman named Chi Hsien. He could tell everything about birth and death, gain and loss, misfortune and happiness, and the length of a man's life, predicting the exact year, month, week, and day as though he were a god. The people of Cheng used to flee at the mere sight of him. Lieh Tsu went to see him and was fascinated. On his return, he said to Hu Tsu, "Master! I used to think that your Tao was perfect. But now I know something more perfect still."

Hu Tsu said, "I have taught you only the letter and not the spirit of Tao. Do you really think that you have mastered Tao? If there is no rooster in a flock of hens, how can they lay fertile eggs? You try to flaunt your knowledge of Tao to make people believe in it.

That is why people can see right through you. Bring the shaman here and I will confront him."

The next day Lieh Tsu brought him to see Hu Tsu. As the shaman left, he remarked, "Alas! Your master is dying. He will not live another ten days. I saw something strange in him. He had the appearance of wet ashes."

His gown drenched with tears, Lieh Tsu went in and told Hu Tsu what he had heard. Hu Tsu said, "Just now I showed him the still and silent earth, the tranquil and motionless mountain. Probably he saw only that I have dammed up the springs of my vital energy. Bring him back again."

The next day the two came again to see Hu Tsu. As the shaman left, he said, "It is fortunate that your master met me. He is getting better already. He is perfectly alive. I can see that the closing up of his energy flow is only temporary."

Lieh Tsu went in and told Hu Tsu. Hu Tsu said, "Just now I showed him the heavenly void without name or substance. My vital energy comes up from my heels. Probably all he saw was my releasing the springs of this energy. Try to bring him back again."

鄭有神巫曰季咸知人之生死存亡禍福壽夭
期以歲月旬日若神鄭人見之皆棄而走列子見之而心醉
歸以告壺子曰始吾以夫子之道為至矣
則又有至焉者矣壺子曰吾與汝既其文未既其實
而固得道與眾雌而無雄而又奚卵焉
而以道與世亢必信夫故使人得而相汝嘗試與來以予示之
明日列子與之見壺子出而謂列子曰嘻子之先生死矣
弗活矣不以旬數矣吾見怪焉見濕灰焉
列子入泣涕沾襟以告壺子壺子曰鄉吾示之以地文
萌乎不震不正是殆見吾杜德機也嘗又與來
明日又與之見壺子出而謂列子曰幸矣
子之先生遇我也有瘳矣全然有生矣
吾見其杜權矣列子入以告壺子壺子曰鄉吾示之以天壤
名實不入而機發於踵是殆見吾善者機也嘗又與來

The next day the two went again to see Hu Tsu. As the shaman left, he said, "Your master is never the same. I have no way to read his face. Wait until he settles down, then I shall examine him again."

Lieh Tsu went in and told Hu Tsu. Hu Tsu said, "I have just shown him the ultimate harmony, where there is perfect balance. Probably all he saw was the depths of my vital energy in its perfection. When the waves swirl in a torrent, there are dark depths. When the water is still, there are dark depths. When the water flows, there are also dark depths. There are nine names for the dark depths. I demonstrated only three of them. Try to bring him again."

The next day the two came to see Hu Tsu again. Before they even sat down, the shaman lost his nerve and fled. "Run after him!" Hu Tsu said. Lieh Tsu ran but could not catch up with the shaman, so he returned and said to Hu Tsu, "He has disappeared. He is gone. I could not find him."

Hu Tsu said, "I just showed him what existed before the beginning of things. Completely open and yielding, I showed myself, without a care, like grass bending before the wind and water flowing in waves. That is why he ran away."

Whereupon Lieh Tsu realized that he had not yet begun to understand. He went home, and for the next three years he did not go out. He did the cooking for his wife and fed the pigs as though they were human. He took no interest in worldly affairs. He stopped making complications and returned to simplicity. Rooted in the earth and centered in his body, amid all the confusion and distractions of life, he remained one with Tao until the end of his days.

Do not seek fame. Do not make plans. Do not be absorbed by activities. Do not think that you know. Be aware of all that is and dwell in the infinite. Wander where there is no path. Be all that heaven gave you, but act as though you have received nothing. Be empty, that is all.

The mind of a perfect man is like a mirror. It grasps nothing. It expects nothing. It reflects but does not hold. Therefore, the perfect man can act without effort.

南海之帝為儵、北海之帝為忽、
中央之帝為渾沌。儵與忽時相與遇于渾沌之地、
渾沌待之甚善。儵與忽謀報渾沌之德、
曰、人皆有七竅、以視聽食息、
此獨無有、嘗試鑿之。
日鑿一竅、七日而渾沌死。

The ruler of the South Sea was called Light; the ruler of the North Sea, Darkness; and the ruler of the Middle Kingdom, Primal Chaos. From time to time, Light and Darkness met one another in the kingdom of Primal Chaos, who made them welcome. Light and Darkness wanted to repay his kindness and said, "All men have seven openings with which they see, hear, eat, and breathe, but Primal Chaos has none. Let us try to give him some." So every day they bored one hole, and on the seventh day, Primal Chaos died.

A NOTE ABOUT THE TRANSLATORS

Gia-fu Feng was born in Shanghai in
1919, was educated in China, and came
to the United States in 1947 to study
comparative religion. He holds a B.A.
from Peking University and an M.A.
from the University of Pennsylvania.
He has taught at the Esalen Institute,
Big Sur, and now directs the Stillpoint
Foundation, a Taoist community in
Manitou Springs, Colorado. He is the
author (with Jerome Kirk) of *Tai Chi—
A Way of Centering—& I Ching,*
which was published in 1970.

Jane English was born in Boston in 1942.
She holds a B.A. from Mount Holyoke
College and has received a doctorate from
the University of Wisconsin for her work
in high energy particle physics. She has
taught a course in Oriental Thought and
Modern Physics at Colorado College,
with Gia-fu Feng as guest lecturer, and
is codirector of the Stillpoint Foundation.

The present book, Chuang Tsu/*Inner
Chapters,* is a direct outcome of the
successful collaboration between Gia-fu
Feng and Jane English on Lao Tsu/*Tao
Te Ching,* published in 1972.

A NOTE ON THE TYPE

This book was set on the Monotype in Centaur, a type face designed by Bruce Rogers (1870–1957) and adapted by him for machine composition in 1929. It is the only type face designed by Rogers that is available for machine typesetting. The letter forms are based on the type face used by the Venetian printer Nicholas Jenson for his edition of Eusebius in 1470. Centaur is lighter in color than the Jenson type and has sharper serifs, but it preserves both the generously wide letter forms and strong sense of the calligraphic tradition that characterize the Venetian type faces of the fifteenth century.

Composed by R.R. Donnelley & Sons, Co., Chicago, Illinois. Printed and bound by Halliday Lithograph Corporation, West Hanover, Massachusetts. Typography and binding design by Clint Anglin.